TABLE MANNERS

TABLE MANNERS

BY MARTY GERVAIS

mosaicPRESS

Library and Archives Canada Cataloguing in Publication

Gervais, C. H. (Charles Henry), 1946-
[Poems. Selections]
  Table manners : selected and new poems, 2004-2018 / Marty Gervais.

Issued in print and electronic formats.
ISBN 978-1-77161-342-2 (softcover).--ISBN 978-1-77161-343-9 (HTM-
L).--ISBN 978-1-77161-344-6 (PDF).--ISBN 978-1-77161-366-8 (Kindle)

I. Title.

PS8563.E7A6 2018   C811'.54   C2018-902069-5
                                                C2018-902070-9

Published by Mosaic Press, Oakville, Ontario, Canada, 2018.
MOSAIC PRESS, Publishers

Copyright © Marty Gervais 2018
Edited by John B. Lee
Design By Courtney Blok
Cover photograph by Marty Gervais
Printed and Bound in Canada

ONTARIO ARTS COUNCIL
CONSEIL DES ARTS DE L'ONTARIO
an Ontario government agency
un organisme du gouvernement de l'Ontario

We acknowledge the Ontario Arts Council
for their support of our publishing program
We acknowledge the Ontario Media Development Corporation
for their support of our publishing program

Funded by the   Financé par le
Government   gouvernement
of Canada   du Canada   Canada

MOSAIC PRESS
1252 Speers Road, Units 1 & 2
Oakville, Ontario L6L 5N9
phone: (905) 825-2130

info@mosaic-press.com

Other Books by Marty Gervais

Poems for American Daughter, 1976

Into a Blue Morning, 1982

The Fighting Parson, 1983

Letters from the Equator, 1986

Autobiographies, 1989

Scenes from the Present: New Selected Poems, 1991

People in Struggle: The Life and Art of Bill Stapleton, 1992

The Border Police, 1992

Playing God, 1994

Seeds in the Wilderness: Profile of Religious Leaders, 1994

From America Sent: Letters to Henry Miller, 1995

Tearing into A Summer Day, 1996

The Science of Nothing, 2000

To be Now: New and Selected Poems, 2003

A Show of Hands: Boxing on the Border, 2004

Reno, 2005

My Town: Faces of Windsor, 2006

Lucky Days, 2009

Afternoons with the Devil, 2010

Ghost Road, 2012

Touch the Darkness, 2015

Five Days Walking Five Towns, 2017

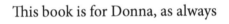
This book is for Donna, as always

ACKNOWLEDGEMENTS

I write in the early morning hours at Tim Hortons near my house. A handful of sleepy souls pore over the papers scattered across the tables. My routine is set: order steeped tea, and a toasted bagel, track down *The Windsor Star* tucked secretly away under coffee supplies behind the counter, because the staff fears the Chrysler workers nearby will steal it, then I head to my table in the corner. It is there that I write. After years of working amidst the constant clatter of a newsroom, I seek refuge in a noisy coffee shop, and bless its kindly employees for taking care of me. But there are so many people over the years that need thanking. John B. Lee, who edited this volume, has been my best editor, honest and wise in his criticism. Loyalty, too, is something that's important, and that I find in Howard Aster at Mosaic Press. His continued and unwavering support over the years is the greatest gift of all. I also thank Matt Goody at the press for his enthusiasm for this next chapter in my poetry. Also, I am grateful to the City of Windsor for permitting me to serve as the city's first poet laureate, and keeping me doing that for seven years. It opened my eyes to so many untold stories from this part of southwestern Ontario. I also need to single out the editors and poets who have encouraged me, offered advice, and sometimes left me with their criticism that kept me awake at night worrying about whether I should rewrite a particular stanza. These include Dan Wells, Robert Hilles, Karen Mulhallen, Rosemary Sullivan, Phil Hall, Bruce Meyer, Roger Bell, Mary Ann Mulhern, and Peter Hrastovec. Many thanks, too, to Laura Mulrooney for the early preparation and compilation of this manuscript before editing and Kerrisa Drouillard for last minute proofing. Finally, I need to acknowledge my family, especially my wife, Donna, for giving me the time to daydream and fall asleep on the couch in the middle of imagining new poems.

Table of Contents

My Wee Friends
Barber Shop in Iraq
That Day at War
Nothing to Fear
Change at the South Beach Cafe
The Blue Lady
The Treasure
We Used to Ride to California
Is That My Heart?
Taking My Blood
The Angel at My Bedside
As the World Turns
The Man in the Next Bed
The Red Ribbon
Turning Back the Clock
Sunday Crossword Puzzles
Imagine Myself Bearing Good News
The Lexicon of Snoring
The Cow in Your Kitchen
Loose Fitting Light

From *Touch The Darkness* **:: *111***

River Poet
Hands
Those First Days
To Touch the Sky
The Wedding Dress
Summer Nights Outside Metropolitan Hospital
The Old Man's War
Running From Us
Upside Down
The Magistrate's House
Our Canadian Flag Along Detroit's Shore
Cathedrals
Moments Before the Old Presses Started at the Windsor Star
Stables at Kenilworth Race Track
Agnes At Rosa Parks/ West Grand Blvd.
Summer in Detroit
Einstein's First Concert
Upon Joe Frazier's Death
Porch Spiders
Mr. McLuhan and the Windsor Cow

But who says this is true

Marty Gervais is a poet who knows the value of a good story and he proves himself in every poem in this collection to be nothing short of a master storyteller. His poems honour the narrative impulse set in lyrical form. And he is often something of a mischief maker in that he frequently writes with a twinkle in his voice, teasing the truth out of sometimes peculiar experience. He is a confabulator who makes one think *pity the poor historian* adhering slavishly to the dull plod of facts. But when the facts serve the truth they come embraced in varity. His poems revel in humour, invention, and wonder, for *his* is the sagacious tease of the wise fool. We all have a favourite author who enlightens and enlivens, entertains and teaches, giving us the gift of sacred truths along the way. He is by times the court jester and by times the court poet lifting his more serious voice in song. We may look to him for the art of wishful thinking. We may look to him for the lessons of the parable and for the keen eye of the reliable observer. If we pay close attention we find those phrases that lift the hair on the nape of the neck and deliver the frisson of delight when the poet's language has the rhetorical dash of genuine music in the line. Consider then Gervais' lovely phrasing "Time is a fugitive/ in a landscape of fancy," from his poem "Turning Back the Clock". And know - this is the work of a major poet at his best.

Gervais is an important practitioner of the tradition of Peoples Poetry. Both as a publisher and as an author he has always been something of a champion of poetry that is actually about something. A highly deserving recipient of the prestigious People's Poetry Award, Gervais confirms his place as one of the most gifted poets working in that tradition. *Table Manners* gives the reader the affirmation that when poetry has content that is both deeply moving and profoundly intelligent, when it serves deep need and it stirs the common feeling of what it means to be fully human. We might carry these poems with us into the future, folded up in our wallets, committed to memory, remembered and cherished and we might buttonhole friends and strangers and say, "Just listen to this:"

Let me try again
Let me make it up
Let me imagine
something better
Let me find some joy
search their eyes
touch their lips
comb their hair.

These lines from Gervais' poem "Barber Shop in Iraq," are worth the price of admission into the world of Marty Gervais. Imagine this. Remember this. Dream this. Say this of me. "They have all the answers," he writes in "Sunday Crossword Puzzles," "I only have questions."

"What do you know," he asks of his hands in his poem "Piano Hands." "It wanders by itself/ seeking wisdom or truth/ the eye with the mind of its own," he writes of his own rogue eye. "Hey lady, how does this thing work?" he quotes a grandson frustrated and disappointed by the magic wand that fails to dazzle and amaze. It's a dud and his grandson feels cheated. There's laughter in this, and wisdom and a clear understanding of the imagination of a child discouraged by the discovery that the wizard's wand is just a painted stick.

Marty Gervais is a poet of black cats, lucky chestnuts, smashed eggs, magic cows, headless chickens, garrulous monks, wolf soups, hospital dogs, blue ladies, upside down cities, and at one point he closes a poem saying "I'm everybody." And the breadth of his imagination, the quality of his mind does not end with the odd or the strange. It is perhaps at its most moving when he writes about his family. Notwithstanding the wry humour of that disappointed grandson, the reader is also treated to the mystical appearance of his grandparents ghosts in the landscape of the family farm in the French region of southwestern Ontario. We also see how a sunny summer day spent poolside at his suburban home in Windsor might suddenly turn tragic when a grandson falls into the deep blue water and drifts dreamily to the bottom … the poem begins "The pool lay/ like a sweet blue sky/ in the advent of summer" and it transforms into "…the blue torment" with his son the hero rescuing the boy "I saw tiny thin arms wrap tightly/ around my son's neck/ I saw the boy's face swimming/ in tears of sunlight." In "Breathing Sweet Hope," the poet as god writes "I will stop time/ - here and now - to move/ all these pieces into place/ the perfect farm/ in this imagined game/ I will open the eyes of those I love/ and breathe sweet hope/ into their limbs and words/ I will let prayers/ finally have their day". In the poem "Plotting My Way Home," the humble poet acquiesces "But who says this is true" … plotting his way home in a studied avoidance of black cats, almost believing in the supernatural powers he surrenders to the possibility that the pesky black cat might possess the ability to "unleash a host/ of unfortunate events." Who says this is true, indeed! For his part, the persona in the poem goes searching alternate routes "desperate to find any other way home." We are there with him in the early morning light, there with him at sundown, there with him at the coffee shop and in the press room at the newspaper, there with him at a family gathering, and there in the city where he is Poet Laureate giving the city meaning, gravitas, humour and wisdom in full gulps. *Table Manners* ends with these wise words "turn your faces to the night/ forget everything/ let it go." And so we surrender and begin again to "study the ants … in the light of an ordinary morning."

John B. Lee Poet Laureate of the city of Brantford in perpetuity Poet Laureate of Norfolk County for life

Wait For Me

In The Light of An Ordinary Morning

I study the ants
swarming the counter tops
in the light of an ordinary morning
Some march in single file
others in twos
Some pause momentarily
remembering suddenly
they left behind their wallet
or prescription
on the dresser at home
Some stand stock still
maybe waiting for a friend
maybe talking on the cell phone
Some scurry like they're late
for an appointment
Some walk in circles
confused and desolate over
a bad piece of news
A dab of strawberry jam
is the prize, the mother lode
It sits on the cutting board
amid toast crumbs
and the engineers are drafting
a strategy to spirit this
to the nest, to the Queen
who paces in front
of a tiny ant mirror
despairing over the weight
she's put on and what
she'll wear for the feast
celebrating their great find
I'm way ahead
I know something they don't

I know it's a matter of time
before I wreak havoc
upon this industrious colony
What shall it be?
Flood from an overturned mug?
Tsunami by wash cloth?
Death by a giant finger
flicking them into insect eternity?
Or should I be the benevolent god?
I'm way ahead —
Let them live an hour longer
while I drive to Home Hardware
and buy those tiny plastic
feeding stations
— space age looking drive-ins
I'll invite them one by one
to pull into these rest stops
along their route
to gorge themselves
on super-sized meal deals
I'll give them time to go back
and tell friends
and bring the little ones,
the old, the sick
I'm way ahead of them
God is good
God is patient
God feeds his children

Taking A Drive On Summer Evenings

He tells me that
on summer evenings
he cruises by the house
owned by the man who slept
with his wife
and slows down in uncertain hope
of hearing this man's voice
through the screen door
spying him cutting
the lawn, or fixing his van
It doesn't bother him like it used to
There was a time he would avoid
driving in that end of town
take a detour
and if he had to run by the street
where this man lived
he would look the other way
maybe turn up the radio
maybe talk loudly to himself
Now he makes a point of
going out of his way
like visiting a grave site
of someone who mattered
He's never spoken to the man
never dialed his number
never written him a letter
Has no idea what he'd say
if he ever ran into him
though silently in the car
he rehearses that moment
of confrontation
There are times too when
he's written the man's name down
and stared at it, imagining
his wife with this stranger
on late winter nights

when he was out of town
recalls telephoning her once
and how agitated she was
and wondered what he had said
to get her so upset
Or the time he got home
and the door was locked
and she came from the basement
Said she had hired a man
to fix the locks on the door
and he was now
doing repairs to the dryer
Never thought anything of it
Now he tells himself
it doesn't matter much any more
not like before, not like when
she first confessed the affair
Doesn't matter much any more
Still, as he turns down the man's street
his heart slows and those moments
thunder in his head and his car drifts
in the warm summer evening
and he imagines how easy
how quick, and how perfect
it would be to torch his house

Praying and Peeing

Inspired by a photograph by Robert Doisneau

I am the boy
with the bird on his head
I'm peeing and this damned bird
that has come in through
an open window at the school urinals
won't budge
I wiggle and squirm
hoping erratic movements
will nudge this fluttering angel
but instead its feet shift on my head
like it's standing on a spinning globe
The other boys beside me
peeing at the row of urinals
are all laughing
I begin praying to the Blessed Virgin
Please Mary, Mother of Jesus
the ever blessed and most immaculate
most glorious beyond compare
woman without defilement
who gave birth to God, the Word,
the true mother of God
I love all living things
I know this to be God's creature
Please make this motley dove fly away
Please make these boys wet themselves
from laughing so hard
Please free me finally of these claws
that dig into my scalp
It's the least you can do
I'm peeing for heaven's sake

Blowing Kisses

My dad on a Sunday afternoon
driving his new Chev
blowing kisses at the blonde
stepping out of the diner
on Wyandotte
and she, smiling, and turning
slightly to let the wind catch her hair
Imagine my dad feeling
pretty good about himself
catching one last look
of the blonde in the rear view mirror
and blowing one last kiss
I think of the word "blowing"
the act of one that blows.
A disturbance occurring when trapped gas
or steam escapes from molten metal
a defect in china
hard breathing
and my dad hyperventilating
in his new Chev at the sight
of her, the molten
metal of the fishtail fins
gleaming in the hot sun
the disturbance around
the heart like trapped gas
Blowing in the wind
The answer my friend
is blowing in the wind
The word "blow"
<u>Noun</u> — (1), *a hard hit; knock; stroke.*
The boxer struck his opponent a blow
that knocked him down.
(2), a sudden happening
that causes misfortune or loss
or severe shock.—
His mother's death was a great blow

But the woman at the diner
was no misfortune, no disaster
No great blow or knock
or hard hit, except to the heart
my dad's heart soaring in his chest
that summer day when all
the world talked of Korea
and Ike played golf
The kisses blowing in the wind
The answer my friend is
blowing in the kisses
Blow and blow and blow
blowback, blow-dry, blowfly, blowhole,
blowup, blow the gaff, blowdown,
blow-by-blow, blow in, blow the whole
whistle
blow gun, blow off, blow ball, blow lamp
blowjob, blow hot and cold, blowhard
blow a person's mind
Blow and blow blow
and blow your boat
gently down the street ...
and my dad's car rides
like a boat on the heat waves of suburbia
and he'll huff and he'll puff
and he'll blow the house down
Blow: *a sudden attack or assault.*
The army struck a swift blow at the enemy
I think of the expressions
comes to blows, to start fighting
After a few harsh words
the two boys come to blows
over the sweetheart at the diner
And my dad's car rides proudly
in this big Chev
Blow, blow, blow
I'll huff and I'll puff and
I'll blow your house down

And the newspapers reported
a blow-by-blow account of the day
I think of my dad riding in
his big blue Chev, its fins glistening
and proud in the sunlight
I hear
blow blow blow your boat
gently down the street
I'll huff and I'll puff
And I'll huff and I'll puff
and I'll blow your house down

The Egg
For Pat Sturn

It might've been a cloudy
Thursday morning
as you made your way to school
and scooped up
a speckled blue robin's egg
that had fallen in the field
behind the house
You slipped it into your pocket
and from time to time
throughout the gloomy day
you slid a hand into the warm jacket
and cupped its subtle contours
like a pebble washed ashore
It might've been after haying
and a sky swarming
with black birds and storm clouds
that brought you by this field
and you marveled at
this feather-light egg
and took it home
and worried over its fragility
its glossy membrane
embraced by your hand
like a secret
It might've been
you felt badly the next day
and went back to the raked
and rolling field and stood
under a wide open sky
and, open palm, held the egg up
as if it belonged among the wind
or it might've been your uncle, furious
at your laziness and daydreaming
slapped your side and
broke the tiny egg

in your pocket and told you
to wake up and get back
to your chores
Or it might've been
that every now and then
when you sleep at night
the egg seems to float
in your weightless boyish dreams
sky blue and small

The History of My Clothes

I dress in the dark
so as not to wake my wife
when I get up at 5 a.m.
The pants
I wore yesterday
gabardines, blue,
34 in. waist, 30 in-seam
washable — bought
at Moore's on sale
Was $78, marked down 15%
now another 30%
for the summer sale
I'll wear them again
What about a shirt?
I won't turn on the lights
in the closet — I reach
out in blackness
like a blind man
and feel the lineup
on hangers, convinced
I can match the feel
of the fabric with the colour
I've mastered this
also memorized the order
from left to right:
three shirts in, I'll find
a blue broad cloth
button down, bought
at the Bay three years ago
15 neck, 34-35 sleeve
full price $43
Next to it are two silks
tailored in Hong Kong
very blousy
I won't wear them
feel too much like Mozart
whenever I extend my arms
loose-fitting sleeves drooping
Feel the urge to play — notes

bouncing in my brain and feel
I'm wearing one of those
courtly period powdered
periwigs
I settle on a shirt
counted eight from the left
a *Daniel Hechter*, button down
cotton/polyester blend
robin's egg blue
I could be a stockbroker
— I'll take risks today
buy and sell immortal souls
like Lucifer, make a fortune
for some, ruin others
But first I've got to find
some underwear — *Standfields*
loose fitting, large
I hate anything gripping me
down there unless it's
of my own making
And my socks, black
always black — buy 10 pairs
at a time, all the same so
when they come out of the dryer
hot like croissants out of the oven
there's no worry over matching
Always the same price
three pairs, $9
cotton, stretchy
I'm ready now
I lay out the clothes on the bed
in the dark, my wife still
slumbering, first the *Stanfields*
now the socks, now the *Daniel
Hechter* and stand there a moment
feeling out of place
awkward like a hockey player
lounging about in full uniform
but without skates

Finally, the gabardines
I'm ready —
I feel like me
I am me
I'm everybody

One Eight Hundred

It started with a phone call
a 1-800 number
on television at 4 a.m.
Harry Lorayne's Memory Power
A short guy
with a Brooklyn accent
pacing a studio audience
inviting each one
to identify themselves
by name and occupation
By the end of the show
after he's demonstrated
tried-and-true techniques
of photographic memory
he's reciting back everything
they've told him
I can't sleep
I have nothing better to do
My memory is shot
My mind often goes blank
when introducing my wife
at a party, or maybe
I panic, thinking *This is stupid*
— I can't remember
her name after 30 years of marriage!
So I dial the number
I am talking to someone
on the phone who takes down
my Amex number
It's settled —
Memory Power will arrive
in five to six weeks
Fine — I go back to bed
A month or more later —
I can't remember how much
time has elapsed — I'm up
in the middle of the night
watching television and realize
Memory Power hasn't arrived

I call another 1-800 number
hoping it's the same
but truly can't remember
if it is — and tell
this telemarketer on the phone"
"I ordered a memory building
product from one of your
television shows ..."
"Do you have the product number, sir?"
"No, I don't. I can't remember it."
"Do you have the name, sir?"
"The product name? No, I don't."
"Well, sir, we need the name!"
"You see," I explain, "I ordered
this because it's supposed to help
me remember things!"
"You can't remember the name, sir?"
"That's right — that's why I need this!"
And so the conversation goes
I tell her I remember the show's host
"You know his name?"
"Sorry, I don't, but he was short
and talked fast and had curly hair."
"That doesn't help, sir — we need
his name! Well ... perhaps you
can tell me how long ago
you ordered this product?"
Sadly, I couldn't —
I didn't know the product name
the host's name, when
I ordered it, not even where
I put my Amex receipts ...
I did know there was snow
on the ground that morning
— it must have been winter
I did know that my car wouldn't start
I did know I telephoned the Auto Club
I even remember the name
of the man who came out

to jump start my car — George —
and can't forget him telling me
his youngest daughter
went to the same school
as my boy and she was sick
that day, was throwing up
I did know a lot of things about
that day — my wife's
hair appointment, even the
time, and my oldest boy was
heading for a hockey tournament,
and my brother was going into
the hospital for more tests
I did know it was a crisp morning
I huddled in the cold
on the street beside the car
waiting for George, and
never saw him again after
that day — never even ran
into him at school
I told the telemarketer all these things
and we talked at length
She was patient and listened
I talked and talked
Told her about my kids
how many goals my son
scored last year
how my daughter
was now living in France
how I had just celebrated
30 years of marriage
— she took it all in
never once showing signs
of wanting to end the conversation
Then she started about her husband
how they met at Mardi Gras
in New Orleans, a wild night
where they wound up
at an all-night diner
and talked till dawn

Now she has three boys
all in baseball, all dreaming
of being Major Leaguers
all under the age 8
So there we were at 3 or 4
in the morning playing out
our lives on the phone
to each other, all the things
we liked to do, how much
we loved our spouses, how
we'd do anything for our kids
how we wouldn't ever change
our lives — we'd do it all over again
if given the chance
I asked for her name and she told me
and I told her my name
Finally I said goodbye
That was it ...
All these years later I remember
every detail about that early morning
the time I spent on the phone
with a stranger — I imagined
she was pretty, imagined her
removing head phones
at the end of her shift and
shaking her hair loose and
reaching for her purse
in the bottom drawer of a desk
and slipping on her coat and walking
to her car and driving off — home
to her husband and getting
the children ready for school
making lunches and
kissing them goodbye
then finally climbing into bed
I think about her often
but realize after all these years
— and I swore I'd never forget this —
I can't for the life of me
remember her name

The Headless Bird

My friend tells me
he cut off the head
of a chicken
and the headless bird
raced down the lane
through the gate —
as if it knew exactly
where it was going
and sprinted down
the highway
toward Highgate
where it finally dropped dead
My friend tells me
it fell short of
the *Guinness Book of Records*
that rewarded a
headless chicken
lasting two miles
before it finally gave
up the ghost
My friend tells me
the town's folk
chased after it
laying wagers
on how far it might travel
My friend tells me
it got to the town's limits
and speculated there
was no point going further
figuring maybe the worst
had already happened
realizing it had left behind something
in all the fuss
Meanwhile why is it
no one ever asks
about the head left behind?

What about the
scared sad eyes of the bird?
That stunned look
that sense of panic
like on someone's face
who anxiously fumbles
for a set of keys lost
in a coat pocket
or left on the piano
by the door
Meanwhile there is
that silly puny head
inching its impotent way
still clacking
"Wait for me!
Wait for me!
Wait for me!"

Finding The Indian Ocean

He had always wanted to dip
his toe into the Indian Ocean
travelled thousands of miles
to South Africa to stay with an aunt
planned to motor to the ocean
but she told him it was dangerous
he ought to stay close
ought not venture too far
Instead, he dreamed
of the ocean 300 miles away
his mind swarming with memories
of youth, a summer
swimming out into Lake Erie
to fetch a cow that had toppled in
and drifted out, how he led
this big hulking wet heifer back to shore
Seeing it standing on the shore
shaking itself free of lake water
before waltzing across the sandy beach
like a fat woman at a barn dance
searching for a partner
He had always wanted to dip
his toe into the Indian Ocean
and all one afternoon pored
over encyclopedias and maps
knowing truthfully he'd never do it
and he lay there on a couch
by the window, the soft afternoon
light falling over him
like the sweet voice of a country tune
He had always wanted to dip
his toe into the Indian Ocean
but instead went out to buy
post cards and guide books
and spent his time driving into town
idling in coffee shops, reading

the paper and talking to locals
He finally told a truck driver
who sat down beside him
at the counter
how he had wanted to make
that trek to the Indian Ocean
if only to dip his toe into its waters
Weeks later sitting by the window
at his aunt's house
a truck pulled up to the house
at the edge of town
— that same man
wearing a wide brimmed hat
got out and made his way to the door
carrying with him a bucket
that sloshed with water
and handed it to my bewildered friend
who asked what this was all about
And the man holding the bucket
spoke about having just motored
from the Indian Ocean
how he had slipped
the plastic container into it
and drove straight back to this house
My friend dutifully peeled off his socks
dipped his toes into the bucket of water
and with eyes shut imagined himself
slowly wading into the open ocean
on a cool morning in July
and turning to his wife
said, "It's not so cold, honey —
once you get in."

Reading Glasses

My wife keeps losing
her reading glasses
Buys them by the dozen
knowing if she has misplaced them
they'll be in any one
of a dozen places — the car
kitchen countertop
bathroom commode
near the phone
on the patio table
in any one of four
or five purses
maybe in a winter coat
maybe in the pocket
of a blazer
My wife keeps losing
her reading glasses
She doesn't seem to worry
— they'll turn up
yet she keeps searching for them
usually clutching in one hand
the thing she needs to read
those few lines of a note
left out for her
maybe a telephone number
or recipe or bank statement
My wife keeps losing
her reading glasses
She drives to Zellers
finds a prescription
that fits her eyes
and strolls out in
the afternoon sunlight
with the new pair
tucked away in a purse
in a place she's certain

to find them the
next time she picks up a book
My wife keeps losing
her reading glasses
I can't help but watch her
as she frantically
searches for them
when she's handed a menu
I can't help but imagine
a dozen pairs
folded up and asleep
like tiny quiet birds
awaiting her call

Cutting the Lawn

Maybe you didn't understand your uncle's letter —
him writing about starting the lawnmower
how he had spotted you driving up the lane
getting out, going into the farmhouse
at Highgate weeks after your father's funeral
You sat at the table by the window
with your mother, and a while later
your uncle finally came into the house
climbed the stairs to his room
at the beginning of a hot spring
changed his shirt, lay the wet shirt
on the bed thinking he might get to it later
then went back out to start the lawnmower
but it was giving him trouble
and long after you had left
he had finally got it roaring
and finished the lawn, but sat down
and wrote this letter
about how your mother had already mowed
the lawn four days before
but here he was going at it again
and talked about the puff of black smoke
that issued from the carburetor
after he got it going, talked about
the wet grass, trouble getting through it
You wondered what was on his mind
what all this chatter was about
what he *really* meant
and you searched the letters that looped
all over the page, hen scratch
You didn't get it, did you?
It was really for him, your father
and it was telling him he was keeping busy
he was making do, the farm was okay
though the buildings needed painting
though the land needed new life

though the boots at the side door
that once belonged to him
could never be filled, not the way
they used to be, not the same
and you didn't see that

Pictures in the Shrine at Chimayo

I can smell the flowers
when I step into this
mission church ...
See a woman kneeling
at the communion rail
She has just tucked
a photograph of her brother
into the corner of a
framed holy picture
a brother who died
of cancer two weeks ago
a brother who had
helped her across the
border from Mexico
four years ago, drove
her in a 1972 Ford Pickup
at night, helped settle
her into a small house
here, helped her
find a job cleaning
the church, doing
laundry for the priest
cooking ... Now she
prays for her brother's soul
her hands wrapped
in beads, lips
trembling, and there's
her brother's picture
high up above
a tiny side altar
tucked in with a
picture of a saint
a smiling man of 45
from a time when
he knew nothing of
death, sickness

tragedy ... He knew
life, and took the risk
to bring his sister
and her children here
drove them 378 miles
mostly at night on
empty Mexican
highways ... His sister
sitting up front with
him in the cab with
an infant wriggling
the other kids cocooned
in blankets in the back
of the truck, fallen asleep
under the moon-filled
night ... She thinks about
that now and sobs knowing
the risks he took, knowing
she could never repay
him except for this
— to pray for him
to place his picture there
among the saints ...

Under the Weight of Heaven
For Br. Paul Quenon

You sleep in the tool shed
by the road under the stars
at the back of the monastery
and tell me about the lovers
— the farm boys
with their sweethearts
who steal into the night
when all is asleep here
and park their cars
in the holy stillness
and after a while
quietly drive back out
to the highway
You hear their cars
mounting the hill beyond
and hear them disappear into
the splendid darkness
You sleep in the tool shed
by the road under the stars
and awake suddenly to
an unfamiliar sound
on the road
and look up and see
the enormous shape
of a horse like a mountain
emerging from the mist
in the early morning
but only a horse
a mare that has strayed from
a nearby farm
It lolls about
under the swaying weight
of the heavens
You sleep in the tool shed
by the road

under the stars
and wake to the morning
with the bells beckoning you
to vigils — then you see
this work horse lying
in the dark meadow
and nod to her as you would
a friend, and say good morning
then make your way to chapel
You sleep in the tool shed
under the stars
where the world
comes to you
— silent guests who steal away
your sleep, who leave you
wondering, who leave you
undisturbed, alone
You sleep in the tool shed
under the weight of Heaven ...

Summer Bird Songs

For Elise and André

Every summer we drove north
to a cabin by Three Mile Lake
I'd sit on the dock in the morning
study the fishermen swing
tackle boxes and rods
into the dew-laden calm
see them shove out into stillness
mist rising, my children asleep
in tangled blankets of bunk beds
this, the most perfect time of day
even the reassuring putt-putt
of outboard motors shattering the silence

Slowly the bird songs would come
back to life in trees bordering
this morning lake

I'd spread out the guide books
on the cedar planks of this dock
desperately trying to make
this connection to nature
— plants and wild flowers
I rarely ever identified or remembered
from one summer to the next
the birds I could never spot
songs I could never recognize
One book suggested translating
their songs into familiar phrases
like *Pleased to meetcha, Miss Beecher!*
Pleased to meetcha, Miss Beecher
to describe the chestnut-sided warbler
or *Quick! Three beers! Quick! Three beers!*
From the olive-sided flycatcher
or how about the red-eyed vireo
with *Here I am. Look at me. I'm up here!*

Here I am. Look at me. I'm up here!
Or try the yellow warbler: *Sweet, sweet,*
I'm so sweet! Sweet, sweet, I'm so sweet!
Sweet, sweet, I'm so sweet!
Or how about the California quail?
Chi-ca-go! Chi-ca-go! Or the Golden-crowned
Sparrow? *Oh dear me! Oh dear me!*
Or the Carolina wren: *Teakettle,*
Teakettle, teakettle!

I couldn't be bothered with such tips
Instead I sailed through the morning
blissfully ignorant, content to permit
the rich cacophony of sound
to wash over me time and time again

Nothing Left To Do

For John B. Lee

Your forehead and eyes swim
in the dirty rear view mirror
of the Bonneville
as it moves lazily
in the afternoon swelter
of Alabama —

I sit in the back seat
and hear your voice
saying you never make left turns

I watch your hands caress
the steering wheel
your eyes in the mirror saying *see*
and I see the hood
of the automobile turn
and turn — trained always
to go right, to spin
like the earth around the sun
or better still, like
a dog chasing its tail

We're not getting any closer
Where are we going?

The car moves like
a continent sliding freely
into position

Even your eyes in the mirror
shift to the right, even
your right shoulder dips
down at every turn
and the Bonneville glides
instinctively like a dancer

never losing step
But where are we going?
I follow your eyes
as they search for openings,
streets, ramps, exits, anything
to receive us and the car
keeps on circling like
a somnambulist chasing a dream

We're not getting any closer
But where are we going?
I imagine turning and
turning till we run straight off
the horizon, till we tumble
off the earth, till we fool ourselves
into going left
all the time swearing up
and down it's right
it's right, it's right

Breathing Sweet Hope

I sit in my car
by the side of the road
watch the combine
shave this field of winter wheat
golden and flat under a dreamy
dark summer sky
I am going to make some changes
That farmer will be my grandfather
he will float over
this landscape — straw hat
coveralls, pipe clenched
in his teeth
I will have him wave to me
from where I sit at the road's edge
I will shift the barns
and chicken coop and outhouse
closer to the house
haul out the wagons
and have my grandfather lead
the work horses into the farm yard
I will put back the oak trees
cut down years ago
in that empty pasture
where we picnicked after church
I will be six again
lumber in a summer storm
and hurry my grandmother
across the yard to shut
the enormous barn doors
against wind and rain
I will put laughter
back into her mouth
as she scoops up my limp body
that has collapsed abruptly
because the sky has erupted
into sudden thunder

I will paint reflections
in her glasses that show
wind swept trees
and spooked barn owls
as we race back to the house
I will exchange the words
in my grandfather's frown
as he stands by the back steps
to tell my mother
who has driven an hour
in the still-dark morning
to hear him say
"Ta mere est morte."
Instead, my grandmother
will be in the kitchen
loading the wood stove
and turning to my mother
and holding her for that instant
I will stop time
— here and now — to move
all these pieces into place
the perfect farm life
in this imagined game
I will open the eyes of those I love
and breathe sweet hope
into their limbs and words
I will let prayers
finally have their day

The Tao of Cows
For Marilyn Gear Pilling

The white cows lie in the Burgundian fields
tired of fences, tired of passing cars
tired of the menu of meadows
tired of shooting flies with their tails

A distant storm blinks over the hills
like a bully striding across a school yard

The cows shrug
Weather is never their friend
There's nowhere else to go
nothing to do but sleep and dream
under the summer stars

I want to tell them
from this side of the fence
how lucky they are —
no car payments, no mortgages
bills, schedules, worries
distant wars, infidelities
or lies or the death of friends
or the sins of pride
or finding excuses to leave a party
or arguments that end in bitterness

I want to tell them
from this side of the fence
I envy their Tao, their chi
their simplicity and the way they move
or shift like the clouds above

I want to tell them
from this side of the fence
they are angels in white —
fat angels maybe —

but still angels
and it's alright to be lazy
to be sleepy, to do nothing
but drift and dream
under this French sky
because they are undulating angels
in white who move with grace
and love the world
and can do nothing wrong
nothing

The Outdoor Barbers

I see them in Beijing
cutting hair on the boulevard
in cool morning light
as men and women
in cars or on bicycles
make their way to jobs
as children traipse off to school

The barbers stand
under the ginkgo trees along
this noisy thoroughfare
awaiting customers who will pause
and take their place in wooden chairs
placed helter-skelter and these men
with scissors and straight razors
fan out the bib-like cloth
this miraculous white apparition
that catches in the wind — rounded
and smooth like the top of an apple pie

If you listen closely
you will hear the quick metal scissors
amid the din in the street
like the incessant complaint of birds
the snipping dance about heads of men
who sit patiently, some
even trying to read the paper
as the work is being done

I watch hair tumble around
their shoulders, eventually drifting
to the street like empty words

I imagine wind catching the hair
seeing it ride in the chilly morning
and wonder about it, how it might

graze the cheek of a young girl
who will brush it away
without thinking of its origins

how this hair might drift all day long
high above chimneys and office towers
seeking a resting place

how it might coast through
an open window and collect
on an altar of burning incense

how it might find refuge
in a café maybe in a bowl of soup
where an annoyed customer might
summon a waiter and point to
its presence lying there curled
and warm amid vegetables and fat
and see the waiter whisk
the bowl away and dump it

or finally how it might float for days
before catching on the cotton sleeve
of a street cleaner or maybe settle
on a statue of Mao and finally find its way
over miles to the Great Wall beyond

A Man Killing a Fly

It seems ludicrous
this would annoy me —
I find myself perched
on the can in the bathroom
with darkness filling the house
after a July thunderstorm
and this fly buzzes about

As a boy my hands were so quick
I could scoop flies out of the air
cup them in my palm
feel them nudge and bounce
feel the power in those seconds
before setting them free
I try again — now a grown man
but my hands thrash
at this damn fly as it circles
like a Messerschmitt
searching for greater challenges

I figure if I wait long enough
it will tire and land

I wait and wait till I no longer
hear it spinning about
then spot it idling on the door frame
and slowly lift up from the toilet seat —
gripping shorts in one hand
an L. L. Bean catalogue in the other
— I'm too anxious
I begin swatting the air again
wildly missing my target

Once again I must sit and wait
and chart the course
of this infuriating insect

as it soars away to the ceiling
I sit and wait and wait
and remind myself be patient
breathe, breathe
one, two, three, breathe, be patient

— then hear it, and can't resist
and madly clobber the dead air
of the room with this catalogue
each time the fly strafes
into my sphere

breathe, breathe, one, two, three, breathe
It's useless but I figure I might get lucky
on one of its incessant sorties

I stand there— pants looped
around my ankles
stand there by the toilet—
naked from the waist down
pathetic and fixated — a lonely figure
loath to surrender
like Hollywood's King Kong
— driven mad and wearily pawing
the night sky for
those insufferable planes

Seven Seconds of Wisdom

Every seven seconds
I'm promised lusty images
and only 10 feet away
a woman on a beach in France
rolls over on her back
on a cotton beach towel
— naked breasts upturned
and praising the heavens above

So casual is she with that cell phone
I fall asleep on straw mat
snoring the afternoon away
my mind swarming with images
of topless women shopping

I dream of women idling over
cute little bottles of Dijon mustard
or fine linens or leather sandals
I dream of following them down aisles
trailing after them to parking lots
dream of sitting in the backseats of cars
spying them putting on lipstick
fixing their hair in rearview mirrors
all the while topless and free

It makes me worry for bra makers
forced to make layoffs
pining over lost bra advertisements
and the absence of pages devoted
in the Sears catalogue to bras
—images of perky young women
resting on the edges of beds
chatting on the telephone
lounging about in locker rooms
with other women, casual
and indifferent in bras and panties

maybe conferring about a downturn
in the real estate market
or whether they should order Thai food

Yes, I worry for the bra makers
and lament the new meaning
this brings to one-piece bathing suits

I agonize for the feminists too
when they run out of bras to burn
or bra fitters and their disappearing art

When I finally wake under a blue sky
I yearn to tell the woman near me
all that I've learned in
those seven seconds of wisdom

Playing Blind Man

I am told
I will be blind in six months
if I don't have laser surgery
I figure I'll need practice
I shut my eyes and shuffle about
this two-storey house
stumble into door frames
knock over flower vases
run my head into open cupboard doors
I'm playing blind man

I shut my eyes and journey
through a house I've lived in for 13 years
touch my way through this silly odyssey
trying to understand
what might befall me —

I wonder if I'll ever
get used to not reaching for my spectacles
I've worn since I was six

I shut my eyes
and move timidly through a house
too large to be blind in
struggling to imagine colours
reds and greens and blues
the bright winter wheat
so green in those first days of spring
now turning a deep brown
in late afternoon haze

I imagine a yellow school bus
on a road maybe a mile away
across an empty field
where the barns bob and float

on the horizon like aimless fishing boats
the sweet reds glowing
under a cerulean blue sky

I move like a somnambulist
in a cluttered landscape
that has turned me into a stranger
an intruder, a home invader

I move along walls
refusing to give in, pushing myself
from room to room
the flat of my right hand
tracing edges, corners
my feet moving as if shuffling along
an unfamiliar lake bottom

I'm playing blind man in a game
I can't lose
when all I need to do is open my eyes
the truest of all miracles

I feel my way
down basement stairs
hear a storm rage outside my windows
hear television news
hear the annoying creaking
of an upstairs floorboard
hear the clock in the living room
I count the chimes
sensing how long
I've been playing this game

I finally land upstairs in my bedroom
rest on the edge of my bed
marvel at darkness —
swear I can see fireflies

or splashes of light
from flickering distant lightning
swear I can reach out
and touch it with my bare hands

Lucky Days

First Snow
For Gabe

My footprints in snow
trace the opposite direction
of my son's
from a few hours ago
He was coming home
I was on my way
to a coffee shop
This first snow
I imagine his teenage body
slipping and sliding
from a warm car at the curb
head hooded, long legs
taking icy steps
in one large stride
to the front door
the darkness disappearing
around him as
he made his way
into the house
shoes in a tumble
just inside
I pause and wonder
about his night
the sweetness of hours
left behind
sleepy legs navigating
through family clutter
while I rise and pull on
a hooded sweater
and make my own way
careful to avoid
his path, making sure
not to obscure his
amidst all these comings
and goings
where our footprints greet
one another
under street lights
at dawn

Plotting My Way Home

I minimize bad luck
by avoiding black cats
that prowl
empty streets at dawn
I spot them a half block away
silhouetted by street
lamp darkness
as they cross
before me
like the devil's silent shadow
and I feel myself
manoeuvre the car
frantic for exits
that might spare me
the path
that led them here
I wheel into back alleys
behind sleepy homes
picnic tables and pools
I speculate that making
the sign of the cross
might cancel out
any possibility
of bad luck
I figure if I put the car
in reverse
and boldly cross
over the ill-omened
path of the cat
this might
reverse the luck

But who says this is true
I am also told
in some places
if the cat is politely greeted
or stroked three times
bad luck will vanish
like mist on a sunny morning

or if a sailor's wife
keeps a black cat
to ensure
her husband's safe
return from the sea
or if you cut off the cat's tail
and pass it over an eye
suffering from a nasty affliction
this will restore perfect vision
but is it true if the cat runs
from the person or turns its back on
its own tracks
that this will unleash a host
of unfortunate events

I am not sure

And because of that
I will go through life, fearing
their presence, and searching out
new routes, exit ramps, detours
shortcuts, avoiding them at all cost
desperate to find any other way
of reaching home

Lucky Days

For Stéphane

My son collects chestnuts
to tuck into his hockey bag
for good luck

I told him
Hemingway rolled them
in his tweed pockets
every morning before he wrote
believing the work
would go better

Today in this arena
in the Alsace region
the late afternoon glow
floods the ice
through this wall of windows
and the chestnut trees
step forward to press
their eager faces against
the cold glass
to catch sight of the boy
who claims
he needs no luck

Sweet Blue Sky
For Sebastien

The pool lay
like a sweet blue sky
in this advent of summer
and the boys were running
in the first afternoon heat
after the retreat of spring rains
all trouble put aside
and boyish laughter rose
and innocent eyes drank
in a new day
till everything turned
and I turned to see
the youngest of my grandsons
— barely 3 —
at the bottom
wafting hair floating
like seaweed
outstretched hands
in slow motion
and frantic legs buckling
searching for
the watery limits of a womb
and I could do nothing
but watch
my eyes open, arms limp
and useless
as my grandson
sank into the summer blue
in a summersault
of tiny limbs
Let me move
Let me pluck you
from that future
but the boy tumbled
and rolled away

his trusting eyes open, hopeful
All this in mere seconds
as my son — his father —
cut the surface
to scoop his second born
from the blue torment
I saw tiny thin arms wrap tightly
around my son's neck
I saw the boy's face swimming
in tears of sunlight

Piano Hands

You have beautiful veins
the nurse told me
She unbuckled my left arm
and surveyed the stark
white landscape
of mapped highways
searching for a way in
a place to insert
the juncture for the IV
I had never thought
of myself like that
Why is it my mother
never told me this?
Instead I was praised
for having hands of a pianist
As a child, I'd study them
for hours wondering
why they couldn't play
I'd sit at the upright piano
in the living room
and command them
to play something
anything – jingle, exercise
birthday tune, anything
What do you know?
I'd ask, and my hands
would lie there
inert, disinterested, dumb
You have beautiful hands
my mother would say
— you'll play someday
you'll stand before throngs
and tell stories
with those hands
and at six I'd sit
in front of our towering piano
and pretend

I'd sit up straight
I'd put on a bowtie
my first communion jacket
arrange the sheet music
and let my hands flutter over ivory
like seagulls dipping into the sea
up and down, sweeping over
the white white
my mind lost in the moment
a darkened concert hall
my beautiful hands
redefining grace
a crowd hanging on every note
Oh my beautiful hands
let them hear you
take us away
carry us into beauty

The Autobiography of Mr. Henry

Mornings I wake
to find him skulking about
making tea, finding the paper
between the doors, letting out
the dog, rummaging for keys
There are nights when
I watch him empty his pockets
on the piano by the door
keys, loose change, fountain pen,
a folded over envelope
marked up with phone numbers

I can't help but notice
an untidy beard
and his right eyelid drooping
like a slum-town boxer
a nose broken
in street hockey when he was 12
rings on his fingers
one gold, one silver
and tips of his fingers ink stained
and the childhood scar
on his left arm from
when he reached across
the table to snatch a slice
of roast beef with his hands
and his father slapped him
with the flat of a knife
and cut him accidentally

I know this man
believe I can learn from him
by studying the glasses he wears
the reflection of a room
a dog walking through
photographs swimming

in the dreamy-lensed landscape
of chairs and lamps
a woman in a bathing suit
rushing through
someone in his life
who asks questions
he pays no attention to

I love this man
follow him from bedside
darkness to early morning
streets as he makes
his way to a coffee shop
and sits with a book
wanting to cover his ears
from grating radio sounds

I want to ask him why
but he is lost
in daylight, in routine

I want to tell him things
I've learned
that might change him

I want to slip inside
and view the world
through his eyes
one that is half blind
the other faltering
and blurred by glaucoma
Is it so ordinary? So bland?

I sense him scrawling
something in a notebook
and pull myself up
on the lip of the eye socket
to glean what he's writing

I can't tell you what it is
what language, what
new world he describes
This man must be truly mad
if he thinks such words
will help

A Place Where You Are Never Tired

We drove the back roads
from Petrolia and got home late
from the game and
it wasn't long before
I had fallen asleep
but suddenly was back
on the road again
rushing through farm country
passing dark floating shapes of barns
that loomed large and ghostly
a combine creeping silently
like a house through
the flat, wide fields, a harvest moon
lighting the way, and
I was making good time
to somewhere I can't say
till I came up
suddenly behind a tractor
and a man chewing on a pipe
taking his own sweet time
along the dark highway
a weak light at the back
twittering in the gloom
I wanted to swear at him
for not giving me enough warning
and for going so damn slow
but when he turned down
the gravel road toward a lake
he waved to me
I knew him and stopped
and saw him step down
slowly from the tractor
the familiar tattered coveralls
a bald head glistening in the moonlight
— my grandfather shaking my hand
But this wasn't his farm anymore

It is now, he said, his arm
stretching to define its space
and how the land ran down
to the water's edge
where the work was easier
and the hired hands
didn't mind waking and working
I don't know where it went from there
but when I woke
I swear I was in a place
where you put in
a good day's work

In My Head

They poked at my brain
below the harsh lights
of the basement room
of the hospital
and removed a bird's nest
tucked secretly away
or so my dream told me

That might explain the voices
the songs I heard
in the early mornings
That might explain the insomnia
the sleepwalking darkness
I carried around with me
all these years
This morning they shone
light in my eyes
waking me
and I felt my pupils dancing
along an empty shore
They asked me where I was
what day it was,
I told them
I was in a movie theatre
and today was every day
and they smiled
and I told them the truth
but asked about this bird's nest
I told them I was worried
the birds might want to return
I missed their songs
so earnest and alive
in my head
and the frivolous beauty
that lifted within

Lazy Eye

Don't call it lazy
—it's simply not paying attention
It's looking to the left
when the other's peering to the right
It's looking at the ceiling
when the other's studying my shoes
It's spying a woman
turning the corner
her red hair grazing her slim shoulders
notices her bright blue shoes
the A-line dress
Meanwhile the other eye
spots a headline in the paper
being read by a man in a nearby café
Lazy? No – Curious. Bold. Nosy.
It wanders like a happy thief
down a department store aisle
It wanders like a canoe set adrift
It wanders by itself
seeking wisdom or truth
the eye with a mind of its own

How to Cook a Wolf
After MFK Fisher

You must choose one
from the Burgundian hills
You must name it — something
symbolic, meaningful, ironic
Not *George* or *John* or *Howard*
Wolfie will do
It must fit in a pot
All its limbs intact
It must be a granny cross-dresser
It must have especially big ears
for perfect hearing
It must have especially
big eyes for 20/20 vision
it must have teeth
as bright as piano keys
It must be a charmer
It must have infinite patience
It must thank the woodsman
for stopping him from himself
for saving his soul
And so it goes — the creature
or Wolfie must be content
to sit and wait and wait
amidst sliced onions, tablespoons
of butter and olive oil
heaping helpings of green pepper
chopped fine, large field potatoes,
diced pimientos and parsley
celery stocks, garlic cloves
—this being grandma's soup
for a cold day in the spring
when the poppies bow their innocent
bright youthful red heads
on the quiet hillside

Room 1607

I'm going to heaven says the man
from the bed next to me
in this 4-bed ward
I don't believe you I say
and remind him of how well
his predictions fared
about the Leafs winning
an ordinary game
against a team worse than theirs
You're staying right here
Sad but true
The man directly opposite me
hasn't been out of his bed
for eight days
—he's going to lose his leg
tomorrow morning
I hear the nurses whisper about it
I can't help but hear the rosy picture
his wife paints for him
Another man arrived last night
and can't recall what nursing home
he just came from
So what's my story?
My gut aches
—my body takes the shape
of a fetal curl
I feel I am lying under a cold gray sky
Out of one eye I catch
the wavering skeletal branch of tree
as it sings a mournful tune
just beyond my reach
I'm going the other way
I hold my breath, beat back the pain
and at night when the 6th floor sleeps
against the backdrop of
humming machines and beeps

and footsteps and carts
I wake and rise in darkness
reach for the plastic urinal
that is shaped to fit my penis
and hunch over it and pee
feeling blessed
one thing on earth
still works

Hospital Dog

Someone in the night
has delivered a stuffed collie
to the man in the bed
across from me
—his childhood dog
that sped around
the backyard
in summers
or chased boys
on a ball diamond
near the school
and ran down
to the river
to spook the fishermen
The man sleeps
but the dog stays
wide awake
perched on the windowsill
like a gargoyle
surveying the city
Neither man nor dog moves
The man's eyes are blue
the dog's gray
That night when
I finally fall asleep
the morphine drip
carries me into a field
climbing a grassy slope
above an S-curve of railway tracks
I spot the dog running ahead
the river beyond
I am trying to catch up
my heart thumping
I am out of breath
my legs weary
The dog keeps its pace

weaving urgently
through high weeds
lifting its head
under a gray sky
then pausing before
crossing the tracks
I am not sure
of our destination
I see the man waiting
on the other side
of the water
hear him calling the dog
I don't know why
I pursue the animal
— it pays no heed to my calls
The man paces the shore
impatient and weary
I finally wake to the morning
to sudden sounds
of nurses removing the man from the room
his family following
heads bowed, faces grim
I swear the dog
tucked under the arm
of his oldest daughter
winks at me
as it drifts by

My Wee Friends

I hear the mice
behind the stove
and know I am not alone
It gives me
something to do
something
to mind the time
at this late hour
I set traps
for my wee friends
in a game of wits
we play —
peanut butter the choice
and gently edge
the traps into place
At 4 a.m. when I wake
I check them one by one
— their tiny faces caught
in a moment of terror
alarmed eyes bulging
as if they've seen a vision
I pry back the stiff jaw
of each trap
and drop their
gray limp bodies
into the trash
This is the ritual
they've begun
They get to gnaw
the bottom of the flour bag
burrow into the rice
and cereal boxes
and at the end
of the night
I sweeten the deal
with peanut butter
I'm happy to oblige

Barber Shop in Iraq

Men slump in chairs
along the wall in the barber shop
waiting their turn
I don't have to look
at them directly
from where I sit —
parts of their dark faces
mirrored, a forehead
an eye, a cheek
a mustache, an ear
I pretend to assemble them
a puzzle of humanity
a mystery — one face
stitched together
though their stories are
much the same
death of a brother
at a check point car bombing
another abducted
and driven for two days
in the trunk of a car
a sister raped, a father
shot by Americans
an uncle dead in a house fire
All in this look of grief
I can do nothing about
Let me try again
Let me make it up
Let me imagine
something better
Let me find some joy
trace the life lines in their hands
search their eyes
touch their lips
comb their hair

That Day at War

I had forgotten
until I wended my way
through the streets
in this northern Iraqi city
how as an adolescent
in Bracebridge
we tossed whiskey bottles
stuffed with lit gasoline-soaked rags
at rotted out tree stumps
and ran like hell
and buried our heads
in the snowbanks
feeling a deafening shudder
in the cold earth
We played soldiers
from the Second World War
borrowed jammed German Lugers
defunct bolt action rifles
and stick grenades
— souvenirs from
other boys' fathers
who came home from the war
We crawled through
the wet underbrush
creeping up on
imaginary enemy lines
and once set fire
to a hermit's shack in the woods
along the river behind
my father's factory
until one winter
we outgrew such games
took up snooker
at the pool hall
spent days
in the smoke-filled confines

below main street
and forgot war and terror
Now I walk this market street
in Northern Iraq, listen
to a man telling me how
his best friend's son
was left bloodied
and dead
on the doorstep
of his house
to make a statement
to register fear
to tell the world
And I wondered about
the poor man whose
house we burned
in the dead of
winter, what kind
of statement that was
what kind of war

Nothing to Fear

Kurdish kids on the rooftop scramble
for broken down chairs
and sit near the edge
to watch the boxers
down below in the ring
Both sun and moon
sulking in the sky like distant cousins
mad at one another
for showing up at the same time
in the same place
The stench of burning rubber
fills the darkening air
and the city stretches its tired bones
fearing nothing
and today I strolled through
the market streets
studied the young boys
hawking chickens, watched them
chop off the heads of
frantic birds as their wings
flapped like flags whipped
in the wind
then saw them drop
their weighty bodies
into a sack for the buyers
to carry away home
I spied sheep's heads on a tray
amazed at the lost look in the eyes
of these animals
like children fallen under
the deep spell of a TV cartoon
Now I am standing
on a roof overlooking
an outdoor boxing ring
following these exhausted men

as they move like lumbering
ghosts desperate to connect
And fear is nowhere to be found

Change at the South Beach Café

The men dance at dawn
in the parking lot
outside the Cuban café
in South Beach
one of them shirtless
another, shoeless
Three black women sway back
and forth, and laugh,
one blows a kiss
to the bare-chested man
Inside the café,
Cuban waitresses huddle
over the *Miami Herald*
spread out over the counter
and read about
the immigration officer
who raped a woman
at a detention centre
My day beginning
theirs ending
laughter is loud
so is the music
the floors unswept
and a stray dog marches
through the open door
like the chairman of the board
and no one seems to notice
but the short order cook
whose voice suddenly
silences the din
and the dog quickly gets
the point, and heads
for the exit without a fuss
I see the light lifting
over buildings
and imagine its warmth

blanketing me
this early morning
The café has cleared out
and the waitresses go back
to talking about the story
in the paper
I eavesdrop from the back
I can't understand most
of what they say
but soon lose myself
in their body language
— curled lips, disdainful eyes
hands firmly planted
on gun-slinging hips
Their day is just beginning
and they're already angry
and the café is now empty
and I soon get the feeling
they're now talking about me
My day is beginning
and I'm already suspicious
I'm like the dog
— there's the exit
but when I count up
the coins and bills
deposited on the table
I realize my waitress
left me change for a five
when it should've been for a ten

The Blue Lady

I saw her picture in the dim light
of the farmhouse
and imagined you as a boy
standing on the verandah
and wondering
what had happened to this lady
with blue hair, blue dress
blue shoes, bracelets blue
on each wrist
and how you marveled at
the veins in her calves
and looked up at your mother
a few feet away
and asked her in a five year
old voice: "Why is she blue?"

But last night I fell asleep
and dreamt of her
that aunt in the picture
on the farmhouse wall
a faded black and white photo
and she swept past my bed
paused at the open closet
where my wife keeps her dresses
and wondered if she might
borrow something
She wore a ghostly white face
a black dress
buttons that ran
from the floor to her chin
I saw it drop to the floor
around her narrow ankles
legs pasty white and stiff
I watched her shuffling
the dresses back and forth

in one hand a cigarette
the ashes falling about
"What do you think?" she asked:
"Maybe something red?"

The Treasure

In the morning his bare feet
touch linoleum
toes curling
from the cold
in the farmhouse
he shared with his brother
till his death two years ago
He rises and limps to the window
raises the blind
on a wintry landscape
the road beyond
and studies the farm buildings
like hunched giants asleep
in the darkness
swears he hears the sheep
that so long ago were taken away
and curses now the silence
and pads downstairs to the kitchen
to boil up water for coffee
turns on the radio
to find out what's gone wrong
in the world
Later that day he tells his nephew
heading off to Cuba
that he may not be there
when he returns
reminds him that upstairs
in the farmhouse
he should peel back the linoleum
near his bed, pry back the floorboards
and slip that metal box
out of its hiding place
In there he'll find old coins
and while he's at it
find the place behind the chimney
where he's hidden some bills

"Get that outta the house
before we sell!"
But his nephew does nothing
remembers the story his uncle told
about the farmer who stuffed
his savings into a mattress
and when he died, the place was sold
but everyone knew about the mattress
and the money
At the auction
the bidding for the bed
started at $10, went as high as $500
and the man who bought it
drove away with the rickety old bed
the farmer died in
and dragged the mattress
into a shed and sliced it open
and found nothing
but goose-down

We Used to Ride to California

The man in the bed across from me
stretches — his back and shoulders
a swirl of tattoos
and reminds me
of the weave of a good suit you catch in
the sunlight on the street
and marvel at its fabric for
just that moment
but the pictures here are of death
  — skull and cross bones,
the devil's face, gyrating sluts
swastikas, peyote landscapes
and bikers and blood red moons
and Macbeth's hags

I am in the hospital only a few hours
when Kenny, this ex-biker
begins to parley through the privacy curtain
the nurse has pulled around me
"You should never have gotten up
on that roof!"
I haven't a clue what he's talking about
"You were roofing!
That's how you got hurt."
I wasn't — I'm here
because my gut has given out
The pain courses through
like an electric current
that won't quit
"How long have you lived on Westminster?"
I have never lived on that street
"You made me that beautiful gazebo
and built me that fence."
I didn't — the pain tightens in my gut
I curl up like a small squashed "a"
Demerol shots hardly touching

the edge of the pain
"We used to ride together — remember?"
I only ever rode a motor bike once
That was in Peru with boys
in the streets chasing me
and calling "Padre, Padre"
And I rode from that missionary village
along a dirt road, the coolness
of dusk rushing through
my shirt and hair
and for this moment
I forget everything else
but the pain tugs me back
So does Kenny's rasp
"We rode that fall to California
— must've been maybe 40 of us!
An army!"
It never happened
Kenny believes I am his old buddy
and we live in the same neighbourhood
on Westminster
and now our lives are boring
now and we barbecue
and drink Blue
and watch the Wings
and talk about old times
when the only pain
we feel is a broken heart
or a hangover or a bruised rib
or skinned knees from a fall or bar fight
But now this, this is our new home
—a neighbourhood of sick souls, woeful voices
a world of stethoscopes and blood tests
and wheel chairs and ID wrist bands
temperature takers and charts and X-rays
Our only adventures now are riding
elevators for more tests
the only glory — the

bruises from collapsed veins
from the daily regime of tests
every seven or eight hours
— they come in the night
and you raise your arm
like a dutiful child in the soft luster
of the room and permit them to draw blood
and you fall back into a stupor
Demerol your only friend
making you believe you have magic powers
and I find myself like a wizard
pointing at my IV pole
making it go right then left then right
again but faster and faster
then it's suddenly doing a crazy jig
and I'm laughing and I'm young again
But Kenny's voice jerks me
back through the curtain
as he rolls over in his bed
and coughs once again
we relive a time — his time —
but it makes him feel good
makes him feel his youth
makes him relive a time
when nothing
ever went wrong

Is That My Heart?

For John B. Lee in response

As I shimmied free
from that tight place
deep within this tube
where a radiologist threaded
a PIC line into the vena cava
a vein that leads directly
into my heart
to facilitate intravenous injections
there was this image
left behind on the monitor
near the ceiling
"Is that my heart?" I asked
"Yes it is." said the radiologist
There it was —
the white dust of light
of my heart and a dark
right lung floating
like two continents
in this sea of emulsion
I marveled at this —
my heart an explosion
of light skimming high
and proud in my chest
my rib cage barely arching it
There it was —
all the things that whirled
within its grasp, the anxiety
from the first moment it leapt
in my yet-formed thin chest
as I spun in amniotic fluids
56 years ago, to the heartbreak
of loneliness, or lost love
or to something so simple
as that fading instant
when I dropped a perfect

fly ball in centre field
in the ninth
and watched a boy of 13
dance all the way home
with the winning run
There it was —
my heart on the monitor
lit up brighter
than the Sacred Heart
lodged in the sweet chest of Jesus
aglow on Lenten cards
There it was —
my heart an eruption of light
gushing through the dusty
windows of your father's barn
on a warm day in October
I reached out to grasp it
and for a moment
I savored it, cupping it
as it burned and sang
in my hand like
a summer firefly

Taking My Blood

At dawn they come
to take my blood
I lift my left arm
and the lab technician
carrying a tray of swabs
and rattling vials
checks the ID wrist band
then feels with her
index finger for a vein
like a blind person
searching features
of a stranger's face —
she gently glides the tip
of her finger over
the snaky blue lines
in my arm as carefully
as my mother checking
for layered dust on the upright
piano top in the parlor
She then slips in
the needle and draws out
three ml. quietly, methodically
Done
Says nothing
Slips out of the room
like an apparition
I hear the rain
on the window
a woman coughing
machines chirping
the ice machine humming
nearby — first noises
of morning
and imagine my blood
in three vials sitting up
in that cluttered plastic tray

proud eager children
as they wend
their way down
unfamiliar halls
like narrow veins
shifting down the tubes
down an elevator
along a narrow passageway
through the lab door
there to rest
my name is stenciled
on stickers —
There they'll find things
about me without ever
asking how I feel
At dawn they come
to take my blood
and I feel a part of me —
tacit and red — slip out
day after day, repeated
like lyrical refrains
day after day bouncing around
in one's head like
soothing melodies

The Angel at My Bedside
for Stéphane

The pain tightens in my gut
I can't sleep
my eyes are shut
I hear someone stir
believe it's the man
in the bed across the room
stare into the darkness —
A dark figure looms
tall and lean poised
at the foot of my bed
Is this the angel of death?
I muse, but look closer
Make out red stitching
on a black jacket
Notice the letters *Flyers*
my six-foot son hovering
over my bed, whispering
something before placing
a cold puck into my right hand —
"A hat trick tonight, dad!"
I smile and place the puck
on the pillow beside me
and fall into a dream
of boyhood in a city
up north when my body
moved with strength
and readiness on the ice
or so I believed
and believe now
again

The Man in the Next Bed

The man in the next bed
has just returned from surgery
and can hardly raise himself up
Finally struggles
to edge himself close
to the side
to pee
I hear the steady stream
puddle at my feet
just below the loose curtain
that divides us into
a semi-private
We face one another
behind the patterned cotton
I can't see him
He can't see me
I don't know his name
The nurse calls him *Sweetie*
He doesn't know my name
My nurse calls me *Dear*
Soul mates
and this puddle at our feet
Pleased to meet you

The Red Ribbon
For George E. Lee

I have tucked this red ribbon
inside my black notebook
jottings about life
on the hospital ward
the nurses
visits from the surgeon
advice from the nutritionist
I scribble out all the meds
given to me, the frequency
potential side effects
Note all the blood work
done, the CT scan
X-rays and white blood cell scans
The red ribbon sits there
day after day — sent to me
by a Highgate sheep farmer
as a bookmark
First prize
Wallacetown Fair
Doesn't say which year
Doesn't say for what
I never win first prize
only ever second or third
or worse honorable mention
A watercolour when I was eight
fetched honorable mention
at the C.N.E.
It was dreadful —
a picture of a fellow fishing
along the Detroit River
He looked disfigured
Judges deemed it "inventive"
Now I have a first prize ribbon
from a town I know nothing about
a fair I've never been to

First prize
a shiny red ribbon
I imagine wearing proudly
strolling amid the bustle
of farmers and housewives
flashing my first prize ribbon
pacing aisles of the best
apple pie, largest pumpkin
longest cucumber
standing about as 4-H club boys
and girls guide sheep and cows
one by one to parade
in the sunlit show grounds
of Wallacetown —
A Ferris wheel spins against
the blue sky, balloons
drift above the din
I walk about with my red ribbon
first prize winner
top of my class
best of the best
my chest sporting the purest
red flower of Agricultural Fairs
I saunter into an exhibition hall
with rows and rows of cages
— chickens and roosters
winners and losers
red, blue, and yellow ribbons
festooned like Christmas lights
to narrow cages —
I think this is me
I walk about with my red ribbon
till I spot the losers — big sad eyes
of these birds
bewildered also-rans
melancholy shut-ins
and know I am one of them
I pick the best of the worst

— a dull white hen
with a gimpy leg
I love her eyes
mawkish and anxious
like women on 1960s
television's *Queen for a Day*
I love her eyes
and when she turns away
I quietly affix this radiant red ribbon
to her rickety cage

Turning Back the Clock

Saturday night and
the clocks already are
turned back an hour
— this trick with time
every fall to give us
a longer day of light
My twelfth night on this floor
nurses with stethoscopes
flying up and down
halls, patients
wheeled up from Emergency
patter near elevators
visiting hours done
The clock looms large
at the nursing station
set back an hour
I want to buy back time
take back two weeks
of a hospital bed
hours of lying
in silence, gripping
my gut, the minutes
stitching my afternoons
into endless streams
of daylight and twilight
I yearn to be
with my 12-year-old son
as he fits together
a toy motorcycle
eyes and hands moving
like the exactness
and polish of a dancer
over these plastic pieces
His eyes dream
this plastic bauble
into something powerful

its thrust and speed
as it thunders down
a narrow street
Time is nothing
for him as he soars
beyond concrete walls
and X-ray machines
hospital beds, labs
and operating tables
Time is a fugitive
in a landscape of fancy
I drift with him
high above smoke stacks
and parking lots
and a city with
minute hands of every clock
clicking backwards

Sunday Crossword Puzzles

My thirteenth day
a Sunday
the *New York Times*
scattered across the table
I keep the lights off
in the room
I envy those who do
crossword puzzles
it's too much like
trigonometry
I can't spell the word
I forget appointments
barely remember
people's names
yet I know all their stories
I can tell you about
the nurses, their kids'
ages, the one boy
born on Devil's Night
the one with a 13-year-old daughter
who has gone to Thailand
to live with her father
the nurse whose father is sick
in the room next to mine
and how she worries
and silently weeps over his stay
I envy those who do crossword puzzles
lining up letters and words and
meanings like Lego bits
fitting their world together
in perfect harmony
lives settled and ordered
unravelling in the across column
like words *for dog's foot*
Muslim monks, bring
the bacon, a Swiss river

a long nosed fish or
the down column
blue bloom, old typewriters,
young pigs, heating lamp
kissing cousins
They taste the
words, the language
and rigorous but fluid symmetry
of nouns spilling over adjectives
They seem to have
found an ordered universe
complete and fortified
as they square in a letter here
erase another, and words
readily dropping into position
like naked bodies spooning
or geese falling in formation
I envy those who do
crossword puzzles
They have all the answers
I only have questions

Imagine Myself Bearing Good News

At dawn, the corridors are silent
and I wander the hospital
I get off at the second floor
see the north wing entrance
draped with Do Not Enter tape
the nursing station abandoned
metal racks now empty of
patients' binders
the wing now shut down
lights dimmed

I am walking at the bottom of the sea
imagine the drift and heave
of plant life, pyramids of form
eerie fish drifting in slow motion
in this muted ballet of form and ritual
The doors to rooms are opened
wide like forlorn outstretched hands
of the souls of purgatory or barn
doors left swinging in a storm or
entrances of a wrecked ship lodged
in the havoc of sand

I am walking at the bottom of the sea
alone and silent among the dead
a place of faint memories
extinct clangor of rolling carts
breakfast trays and footsteps
amid hushed prayers of the ill

I move from room to room
— a visitor, a stranger, a friend
imagine myself carrying daffodils
imagine myself bearing good news
imagine myself bringing life
to all that seemed doomed

I am walking at the bottom of the sea
I have no answers, no questions,
no voice, no name
My eyes wildly search the rooms for clues
My hands collapse and join the silence
My legs are numb and will not move
My heart swims above me
like a face I ought to know

The Lexicon of Snoring

We lie side by side
in hospital beds
opposite one another
He tells me my snoring
is like a battered room
air conditioner kicking in
from time to time
I tell him his snoring
is like a fishing boat
yawing in a stormy harbour
We blow and grind
in our own ways
like lazy whales uneasy
and aimless in the north sea
We sputter like Spitfires
in our sleep, the rising
and falling of guttural
noises, diving low and
soaring high, bombing
villages and factories
and dogfighting enemy
planes and bearing
the babel of sleep from deep
within us, nightmares
dreams, hopes, regrets
the overtures roll like
tumbleweed across
an open prairie
and we're running
into the wind as the
sky swirls into a storm
all black and gray
like a bruise on
the arm, and we
feel the headlong
day and the tide
of the moment
We snore like politicians
on the hustings
making sense of nothing

blather and jabber
in the chaos, and go right on
caring nothing if anyone
hears our message
We snore and we snore
and we snore like evangelists
flipping frantically for
the right chapter and verse
then sputtering it out
in pressing and insistent refrains
We snore and we snore
and we snore in
prolonged stretches
like a breakaway
to the net, our bodies
poised and never yielding
till that precious moment
when we let the puck fly
into the twine
We snore and we snore
and we gasp and we puff
and we heave, lifting ourselves
higher and higher
then sinking and falling
and rising again, slowly
advancing like a huffing
steam engine picking up
speed and suddenly roaring
for all its worth and then
we're backtracking
in muffled grunts
like disgruntled old boars
in the yard
and we snore and we snore
and we snore …

The Cow in Your Kitchen
for John B. Lee in Brantford, Ontario

I shuffle back to my room
along tunnel-like hospital corridors
I've been up since 4 a.m.
reading the *Sunday Times*
It's now 5:30
Soon the sun will loom through
the east window slatted with blinds
and nurses will rest a tin bowl
of soapy water on the chair
in the corner where I can wash up
Now I want to sleep
I fall headlong into a dream
— sleeping pills and
Gravol shots finally kicking in
I see this cow in your kitchen
with Carnation Cream cow eyes
blinking at me with big
girlish lashes, and it won't
budge and I call out to you
but you are in the other
room talking on the phone
The cow shifts its clumsy heaviness
and nudges me against a table
I'm thinking why the hell
is there a cow in your kitchen
and what's your family
thinking by having it loll
and laze on the linoleum floor?
Now the cow leans and groans
It's tired and wants to lie down
on the table beside the flowers
I brought you yesterday
It peers up at the clock over
the stove and knows it's time
for its afternoon nap

and bellows out one more moo
before nodding off
The cow is in my way
You don't seem to care
It's part of the family
like a loveable old dog or cat
I watch its big eyes flutter
then finally shut
Now it's dreaming —
maybe going on family picnics
riding in the back of
the truck like an offish kid
with big lips, funny ears
and a weight problem
maybe riding the school bus
getting weird looks
maybe staying up late
with Mom and Dad
watching Planet of the Apes
I sleep and I dream
of your cow and its dream
as it muses over its happy
contented life in Brantford, Ont.
where it's not uncommon
to have a cow as a family pet

Loose Fitting Light

Home —
yet patches of light
hospital light
sunlight
pools of light
spill into my dreams
I sleep and still see
wires meshed
in strands of illumination
ghost images of the IV
institutional ceiling cracks
stainless steel reflections
mirror glare
dazzling shadows
I see myself running
inside a barn
I see water coursing
from the pump near
the house, light
dancing in rivulets
my grandmother working
the handle, her hips
swaying in loose fitting
gingham, like the light
that flits in the dusty
patterns of this barn
where I run
She is young
I see my mother's face
in hers
I am running in light
patterned on the wide
wooden floor boards of those
barns near Stoney Point
My arms like wings
my mouth sputtering

out sounds of an airplane
as I spin and soar
as I whirl in
this fleeting luminosity
alive in the day
then suddenly
I am older, reaching out
on a ballroom floor
to legs all around me
my face floating
like a sea urchin
in this forest of nylon grace
beautiful female legs
dancing all around me
romping red pumps
I feel pure
I am invisible
My heart pulses
I am in love with
the lights as they play
upon this glistening sea
patches of radiance
I wake with my arms
around my wife
feel the thin cotton
of her pajamas
the curve of her belly
I am home

Touch The Darkness

River Poet

See this river at dusk
— its lake freighters
 moving with grace and precision
to melodies of coming darkness

Say it like it is
Say it now
Now say it the same

Listen to the man on the street
—his family at midnight bedded down
and children fast asleep

Say it like it is

Hear the slumbering Ferris wheel on the river
— like the commotion of muted silence
spinning in the morning light

Say it now

Greet the men and women
who pour out of sprawling factories and shops
heading home to sleep and dream

Now say it the same

Salute the bridge in the morning light
and see how it rouses itself awake
to tell the world it's there, it's there

Say it like it is
Say it now
Now say it the same, the same

Yet why is everyone waiting for the poet

who sings off key
will he say it now
say it the same

Tell us the reason
Tell us the story

Go and wake the poet
who sings off key
tell him to say it now
say it the same, the same

Will he wake the morning light?
Will he wake the falling day?
Will he wake the dying night?
Will he wake the bridge
and factories, and families lost?

Go and wake the poet
and let him sing off key
hear the raspy heart
that gives him speech

Let him say it now
Say it the same
the same

Let the poet wake the day
Let him walk the night
Let him dance alone
among Ferris wheels
and empty lots and soaring buildings

Let him sing off key
at the edge of sleep

Hands

The first
— those that snatched me
from my mother and lifted me
into the light to my father
in a cold corridor
at Metropolitan Hospital

From that point on
my life was one of
adult hands — a school nun
gripping my wrist
as she wielded a leather strap,
doctors tilting my chin, palms
flat against my forehead
to find a fever, the priests'
rough hands offering to place
the host upon my gaping tongue,
teachers sliding my fingers
off a page to check the scratchings
of additions and subtractions

and many years later
my dear mother just before she died
gently cupping my hands
like two tiny doves

assuring me
her hands would bake me a pie

Those First Days

In those first days of spring
the turmoil of cold
throws off its winter overcoat
to let the light lift high
above barns and silos
that ride the landscape
like boats on the nearby lake

In these first days of spring
I maneuver the rutted roads
the back way to Chatham
past La Paroisse de St. Pierre sur la Tranche
where my mother sang
and marvel at how the tall oaks stretch
like boys stirring in the morning

In these first days of spring
I think of that young farm girl
tiptoeing among frantic birds
in the sunlit henhouse
to gather eggs
while my father paced in the yard
waiting for his new bride

In these first days of spring
I recall my own youth —
reckless nights of drinking
my gut aching
as I rode the trains west
through the mountains
believing in all my fears
In these first days of spring
I drive the river road
the back way to Chatham
past graveyards and levelled fields
I yield to the land
as it trembles like an open palm
ready to gather me in its hold

To Touch the Sky

There seems to be
no point — the images
all the same, the words
echo in my heart, my
brain bloated with
the jargon of betrayal
of pain, of things
that make no sense
all the whys —
It's all the same
I'm saying it differently
inventing new ways
to tell you how
the hurt thunders
through my veins

I'm a kid
again, standing in
the schoolyard
troubled by
the unkindness of the
nun who scolded me

I climb a tree and
stare into the
classroom below

the nun's dress sways
like a black cloud on
a summer day
as she moves up
and down the aisles

I'm hiding from her
in this tall straight maple
high enough to

touch the sky, feel the
blueness sing in my
heart, assured
I can taste the beyond

I perch there
on a steady branch
alone, the weight
of her words lifting
from me

Today I wish
I could climb that tree
to taste the blueness
its purity, its
simplicity, to put
away all this heartache
to be a boy again ...

The Wedding Dress

The first time I saw it
I was six
and sunlight spilled
through the bedroom window

I lifted this limp white satiny dress
from a flattened cardboard box
in the cedar chest

I raised it high above my head
— the fitted narrow waist
with a row of fabric-covered buttons
and the invisible side buttons
along the left side seam

Arthur Godfrey on the radio
in the other room
a kettle's whistle
sounds of the man next door
working on the roof of his house

I held the dress high above me
fingers marveling at its smoothness
lost in its whiteness
and the full length skirt cascading gracefully
in alternating tiers of sheer chiffon

when suddenly my mother's voice
at the doorway told me
it was a summer day like this
at the farm in Stoney Point
when first she put on the dress
how she had run upstairs
to the room shaded by the front yard maple

how she remembered
gleaming cars zigzagged in the yard
and her fingers fidgeted
as she slipped on this lacy dress
—the day was hot and cloudless
and her father complained
there hadn't been enough rain
and she told me she had waited
forever resting on the edge of the bed
for her mother to come and approve
and sat staring out the window
shoes resting beneath her
like two sleeping birds
on the hardwood floor

then heard her mother's voice
at the edge of the room
softness of words enveloping her
in that moment

and she knew it was time
to take the car to the church
its steeple towering above the flatness
of farm fields

and she wondered then
if it was all a mistake

Summer Nights Outside Metropolitan Hospital
for Rosemary

I saw my grandmother in the back bedroom
of her little house
She was dying of stomach cancer
I was 10 —
By summer she was
on the third floor of the hospital
I'd visit with my father
but my sister and I had to wait
in the car
We'd roll on the backseat of a sprawling Plymouth
making ugly faces and laughing
or trying to guess which window was hers
We'd wait and wait until my father
would stroll out in the humid twilight air
with ice cream and ice-cold Vernors

After a while we didn't care
about my grandmother
We longed to be pampered
Every day begging our father
to take us to the hospital
We promised to wait by the curb
wait the hours out
for the treats

It all stopped when
my grandmother died

We missed the ice cream

The Old Man's War

The bookshop owner believed
I was blind
I stood in the shop
struggling to make out
the words of De Gaulle's memoirs
reading them in French
I was 14
I had just come from
the optometrist
and the drops in my eyes
continued to plague my sight

I was reading about
the Resistance
and De Gaulle's old mentor Marshal Pétain
reading about betrayal
the decision to save
the aging war hero
who was condemned to death
the decision to exile him
to a windswept island
in the Bay of Biscay

The man in the bookshop
asked if there was a problem
because I held the book
so close to my eyes

I liked the idea
that he believed I was blind
though I never said
anything to suggest this
I went on reading
shaking my head
in modest denials
making him feel sorry for me

I remember this now
as I sit in this cafe

in the Latin Quarter in Paris
and read that someone
has discovered
one street in France
still named after Pétain
in Tremblois
near the Belgian border
— the last town bearing
the former war hero's appellation
soon to be renamed
Rue de la Belle-Croix

A year ago another town
removed a painting of Pétain
from the town hall
I think about this old soldier
called "conqueror of Verdun"
his last days
on the Atlantic coast
a spare two-room bunker
his wife daily walking
from a nearby hotel
to sit and share a meal
and the roll and groan
of the Atlantic just beyond

I remember reading about
his coffin being dug up
and driven across the
country to Paris
where it was later
found abandoned in a garage

Now the modest sign
for *Rue Pétain* marking a street
a mere 600 feet long
is being taken down
sixty years after his death

I wonder about the man
whose final request was
a bottle of water
from Lourdes

Upside Down

It's not a happy face
the shape of this shoreline of ours

maybe it's because
we're upside down
looking north instead of south
like the rest of the country

maybe we haven't learned
to smile so readily —
our weakness betrayed
in that frown

I first heard this
from the nuns in Riverside
at the school two blocks
south of the river

and with my buddies,
we'd slip down
past the heavy sewer grates
and wend our way
underground
down to the shoreline
soaken ankles, wet shoes and pant legs
and emerge wide-eyed
to Detroit's dark smoke-rising signals
that blackened the blue sky

We were a band of boys pretending
to be Tecumseh or Simon Girty
or John Wayne or Gene Autry
The nuns in Riverside said
we were the upside down people

Maybe that's why we did our crazy cartwheels
along the solitary riverbank —
saluting the Americans to the north

The Magistrate's House
for Alexander Bartlet and Thomas Hines

Sometimes I go out
in early morning
cruising up and down Windsor streets
in search of his house
—its sprawling Georgian verandah
the usual sash windows
sturdy front door with transom
and sidelights

They've moved it, but not far
I've narrowed it down
to two or three —
In a way I don't want to know
I want to paint my own story
of that morning: 1865
of the billy-goat bearded town clerk
racing down a flight of stairs
to the landing —
paperboys fanning out into Ferry Street
from the ferry docks
a cold Easter Monday
the boys shouting "Lincoln Shot!"

I see the magistrate's frown
in the dim April dawn
his voice summoning the boys
to bring him the paper
spy him pausing in the gaping entrance
wondering what went wrong
a civil war across the river
the flight of slaves to his shores
now rumours of John Wilkes Booth
making his own run across the river

That Easter Monday
a sleepy town rouses itself awake
to the scuttlebutts
of a ferry boat captain
who stopped at nothing to spin the legend
of being held at gunpoint
by Lincoln's assassin
and the magistrate sorts out
the hearsay down by the docks
wind howling up that street
sweeping its way into the
shopkeepers' doorways
on that spit-gray day

It's all gone now but for that story
and the ramshackle house
that sleeps somewhere
quietly breathing

telling no one
the truth

Our Canadian Flag Along Detroit's Shore
for Peter Hrastovec

If you stand still
you will hear its faint voice
born in winter commotion,
in smoky partisan committee rooms
sprawling auditoriums
Legion halls, and
hallowed parliamentary corridors

You will hear all the good
all the bad, all the everywhere outcry

That was just a little of us
forever trying to make sense
of history, tradition ... and political ego

But its voice was clear—
Let's do the right thing
Let's do it now
Let's hear me sing

A half century later
we sport two broad red borders
like strong shoulders
symmetrical and straight and proud
hugging a single leaf

And here along this river
we might call this a map of anywhere
where the leaf flutters on water
in a peaceful geography of coupling solitudes

I can't help but hear its song calling
This is ours, that is yours
I'll let you see me now
Across the distant shores

Cathedrals

They were cathedrals
—these sprawling factories
with frosted glass metal-framed windows
that tilted open to a landscape
of wartime houses and brick schools
— the workers, like monks, moved
in slow motion, and my father
in a white shirt and crooked bowtie
toiled among them
worried over meeting the numbers

Today, these places lie mute —
edifices of crumbling brick
cracked and broken windows
and the rubble-strewn earth
wrestling back the 20th century
with trees bursting up
through the busted concrete

Months before my father died
we cruised the empty streets
and picked our way among the ruins
of the grand old Studebaker and Ford plants
the Motor Lamp on Seminole,
boarded up dry goods stores
and barber shops and fish & chip joints

We stood in the middle of the sunlight floor
of the place where he made headlamps—
an acre of concrete once complicated
by conveyor belts and sturdy steel columns

and he told me of those mornings
walking to work from Albert Road
chomping on an apple
a metal lunch pail tucked under his arm

a skinny boy of 16 having landed here
from the mining towns in the north
a job on the line, a job he'd never quit
till his heart gave out

Now there are mornings when I pause
before a single building
and peer through a gap-tooth wall
of cracked glass windows
imagining life on that concrete floor

remember him saying he'd trade everything
to return to that time of sweet independence
of youth, a job and a cheque on Fridays

Moments Before the Old Presses
Started at the Windsor Star

The first thing you'd see were
the hands, gloved and ink-stained
then the faces of men dwarfed by
the three-storied leviathan that sprawled out
in the morning ready to rouse and rise

You'd eye the pressmen pacing the perimeter
of this giant and see them stretch long clean sheets
of paper from giant rolls through its idle frame

They knew the monster well and knew
to wait and knew to hear its glory

I used to slide down from the newsroom
to stand nearby and watch, and hear the voices
over the faint growl of this prodigious creature
I'd see them carrying heavy metal plates
clamping them into place, and watch them fit
the curved cylinders to its pulsating contours
— catch the slow mumble among
the men as they moved to feed the beast
to make it come alive, to make it stir

They knew the monster well and knew
to wait and knew to hear its glory

These were the men clambering at dawn
among tiered platforms and galleries
built around this slumbering creature
— the first to spot the headlines
to read the world upside down and backwards

They knew the monster well and knew
to wait and knew to hear its glory

Stables at Kenilworth Race Track

That day driving out
to the tumbledown stables
south of the city
I knew nothing of that moment in October 1920
I'd gone there with a woman I'd met at a bookstore
— horseback riding late, late afternoon
straw and dust and manure
the sharp odour of Absorbine
and tobacco and seeing
threadbare plaid blankets folded over
the gates in the horse barn
and the final rays of sunlight
pouring into the stalls
I watched this quiet elderly man leading the horses
out to the yard, the rich chestnut slope of their beauty
accentuated by the late fall's light

I knew nothing of that moment so long ago
but think of it now, too late,
and realize this man was there —
a boy among the stables
fetching straw and oats
his milky blue eyes and boyish hands
guiding the horses
into the silent moonlit yard at dawn

I want him to be there again with the great ones
— the race of the century
Man O'War and Sir Barton

I want him to be at the edges, slipping past
with pails of clean water
to sense the stillness of the stall
where motionless Man O'War stood
—they say Big Red, as he was called,
was so beautiful it made you want to cry

and say his very stillness was that
of a coiled spring, a crouched tiger
I want to believe Big Red scared the boy
that first morning in the fall
Yet I knew nothing of that day in October
when I drove out to those timeworn stables
where this boy once stood in awe
of men who kept watch over the great stallion

I knew nothing of the track we rode on
at twilight where Big Red once galloped
like a nightmare rolling into history
I wished now I had paid attention
I wished I had remembered what
this man looked like, what he might've said
I wish now we could've talked

Instead, I sat perched on a broken down mare
trotting along a track I knew nothing about
trailing after a new girlfriend
thinking only of her
and my next move

St. Agnes at Rosa Parks/West Grand Blvd.

As night falls, the crack addicts
gather in the abandoned church
at Rosa Parks and West Grand
and piece by piece
they have begun
to dismantle the organ
in the choir loft, ripping out the wood
to feed a mounting bonfire
on the concrete floor —

the towering gothic windows
of St. Agnes bow above
like melancholic ghosts
eager to warm themselves
welcoming these strangers

Someone is singing

I hear them inside
see the fluttering glow
from the windows
hear laughter
broken words of a chorus
lifting in the fading light
of twilight

I see the skeletal tree's tangle
of shapes lurching in my path
along an uneven walkway
to the side door of the church
hear the crackling of fire
alighting the graffiti-scarred walls

imagine a cluster
of men and women
huddling in the cold

I decide to turn back
to the street, back
to my locked car

Seconds before departing
I swear that in the hushed
gloom of the church
I hear the whir
of its big ceiling fans
or maybe wings starting up
coming alive
as voices of adoration and fear
fill the sullen silence of
this wintry city night

Summer in Detroit

A flimsy wooden seat
from Detroit's old Olympia
bought for $25 is the closest thing I have
to the Beatles who played in that arena
once in 1964, again in 1966
and I think of my friend
who said it was nearly midnight
when their Greyhound pulled away
from the Olympia —
the Fab Four singing *Long Tall Sally*
from the open windows of the bus
with teenage girls rushing after them into the street
Cleveland bound, an all-nighter

Someone said they heard their laughter
saw them wave on that humid August night
swore they tossed their cufflinks
to frantic stretched-out hands

My 18-year-old high school buddy
had skipped class
to hang out at the Whittier Hotel downtown
and dialed all day long a radio station
in hopes of winning one square inch
of the sheets Lennon slept on

I don't know if any of it is true
I don't care — the broken down
seat from the Olympia
rests in a corner of my basement

I'm struggling to find some kind of metaphor
for how I should feel, some lyric moment
for this brush with greatness
as I settle down on that wooden chair
the hum of the furnace

in the silence of a summer afternoon
but this is nothing to compare
with the postage stamp-sized remnant
from John Lennon's bed
that rests in a dresser drawer
in an envelope from the radio station

I swear I can hear someone sleeping

Einstein's First Concert

A friend of a friend
had an uncle in Detroit
who remembers
Albert from the winter of 1934

how he meticulously
packed up his violin
before making his way
out to the blue Buick
to drive from Princeton
to Fifth Street, New York

This uncle drove with Albert
— the two in the same orchestra
both violinists
Their first recital
226 paying patrons
Bach's concerto for two violins

This uncle spoke about
Albert's narrow fingers
lifting the instrument
lightly from the case
the bow next
his routine set
a formula of repetition
movement so predictable
as to be perfect
and hopeful as prayer

Albert's eyes danced in
the light of the concert hall
when those first notes rose
and came alive
every sound finding
its place in the silence

Nothing had escaped this man
— not even background radiators
hissing their envy

Upon Joe Frazier's Death
Based on interview with Carl Fussman 2004

I lived by the body shot

My dad
was missing his left hand
and part of his left forearm

I don't know what happened
I never asked

I heard another man
tried to kill him
in an argument
over a woman

I wish I knew now
I never asked

But I got the roof of that left hook
as a boy from pulling
a big cross-saw with my dad
He'd use his right hand
so I had to use my left

I lived by the body shot

My mom? When
your mom dies
so do you ... he told me

I never asked why

Health? You have a
lot of tools in that body —
liver, kidneys, lungs
You soften that up
and see what happens

I lived by the body shot

Medals? I cut up my
Olympic gold into 11 pieces —
gave all 11 of my kids a piece

... It'll come together again
when they put me down

They'll live by my body shot

Porch Spiders
For Calder

For weeks
I have studied them —
at dusk they commence their work
— spinneret magic
fashioning an intricate silken gallery of traps
for their prey

in this night of waiting

first the safety line
then a web of sticky silk
that snags and snares
these bold intruders

I watch these wily orb-weavers
in a night of waiting
feel their patience tested
through a sleepy night
as they doze in silence
dreaming of feasting on everything
that nudges their invisible wall

There's no escaping
in this night of waiting

They sense the vibrations of an interloper
a trespasser having blundered blindly
into its neighbourhood —

In an instant, they leap lightly
through the radial scaffolding
eight eyes, eight legs, sharp fangs
racing for the kill

I wait for these wily orb-weavers

to spin their victims
dress them for death
and wrap them tightly in fine silk

There's no escaping
in this night of waiting

Dinner is served

Mr. McLuhan and the Windsor Cow

Maybe this is what McLuhan thought
when he happened upon
this daydreaming cow
as she trotted
with such thoughtless abandon into
that country road

What was she doing
when there was
nothing else to do?

Conjuring better pastures
maybe ruminating
about meandering into a nearby park
among open car windows
longing for a spot
to snoop and maybe snooze
under a blue Windsor sky

picturing what it might be like
to slip into the back seat
of an old Chevrolet
and doze away the day

There's nothing to do as usual
so why not wander
weary of all that cow inertia
and step out from the others
and leave behind
their annoying bovine gossip
in the lazy humid air
maybe step aside from
that tired list of silly names
Mr. Farmer had christened them:
Devilish Delilah, Crafty Caroline
Pain-in-the-Arse Mary-Rose
and *Ooola-la Ola*

There's nothing to do as usual
so why not wander
where the grass is greener

and why not move gracefully
past the open gate
into that ribbon of road
and break free of the regime
of every day

abandon cow passivity
leave behind a staring crowd

and finally be the girl you always
imagined on those tiresome
going-nowhere days

Coughing Up Jesus

It was the day
my dog ate baby Jesus —
this wiry Jack Russell
knocking the Advent Calendar
to the floor
and rooting out the chocolates
one by one
till the 25th

and Jesus was gobbled up
in that toothy slobbery
mouth of my dog
and the month
wasn't even done—
two weeks still to Christmas
and my dog hacked up Jesus
all up in one rushed instant,
a gooey puddle
sliding like a dark shadow
over the gleam and twinkle
of Yuletide decorations

It was that kind of day

every year the priest
prattling on about
the real meaning
of Christmas
about putting an end
to godless buying
about putting "Christ"
back into Christmas

and maybe that's
what my Jack Russell
had in mind when
he coughed up
the sacred and divine

Squatters

I get out of bed
to see them cavorting
on my front lawn
at not quite 5 a.m.

a mother skunk
and four furry tailed
little ones
frolicking in the moonlight

I regard them
the way others might judge
squatters, or worse,
carjackers

I fear them
I can't say anything

I feel trapped
in my own house
not wanting to risk
making my early morning
run to *Tim Hortons*

yet I wish to warn these creatures
what might befall them
if they dare burrow
under my pool

Last summer
their hillbilly cousins
moved in
I hired a wildlife service
to trap them humanely
failing that fed a hose
down their tunnels

blocking up escape routes
with cement blocks
hoping to roust them
from their home
but they never got the point —

they defied my every move
till I stuffed
their underground grid
with chlorine-loaded pool pucks
and sealed up their exits

Now I want to tell
these happy little creatures
mind your own business
leave me alone
let me go to my car ...
pretty please

Calling My Father

I came across
my father's old phone number
scrawled in the address book

—the numbers rolled off
so easily, the times
I called with
a piece of good news

or that moment
in late spring
when I telephoned
to tell my father
his son, my brother
was dying and
we had better
get down to the hospital

or the call I made
from Vancouver
when I was 20
and needed train fare
to return home
and heard
impatience
in my father's
gravelly voice

I sat and stared
at the number
for a long time
then dialed

letting it ring and ring
wondering if
I should hang up

if suddenly
a stranger answered

Deep down
I innocently hoped
someone
might pick it up
in Heaven

The Timekeeper

My father told me of a man
from the factory —
how after he retired
as the company's timekeeper
he never knew what time
it was — or sorry
that's not exactly true

He told me of this man
who had a dozen broken clocks
in his house
all registering a different time
and he'd go from room to room
scratching his head
wondering which was right
till he decided it didn't matter
— the clocks were wrong
and he'd set them
all at the same hour
never bothering to find out
what the real time was

After a day or two
the hands of the clocks
grew weary and slow
and once again
were out of sync
with one another
and the man would smile
and regard them as old friends
all pacing their time
some running fast, some slow
some no longer caring
to keep up

But the man was patient
and he'd set them all over again
going from room to room
caring for them like stray cats

My father told me
when finally the man died
at home in his bed
the ambulance attendant
scanned the room
to record the time of death

and all the ticking clocks
began to chime in unison

A Blind Routine

Mornings when my father leaves the house
he bids her goodbye —
tells her where he's going
what he's doing
and why —

and swears he hears her
moving about the kitchen
though she passed away
a year and a half ago

He cares not to see
refuses to walk with a white cane —
his world a blur
a slowing pace

Mornings my father leaves
tucking stiff bank books into
bulging pockets
shuffles to the street
to a nearby bank
waiting for it to open

My father has not forgotten
what he promised her
why he's there
and finally slips behind a desk
and directs the clerk
to scan the columns
recite its debits and balances
He nods and bids
the kind woman — adieu
His world a blur
a slowing pace —
of greetings and goodbyes

My father has not forgotten
the weight of keys
in his pocket for a
car he no longer owns
Some afternoons
he falls asleep in a chair
cupping the keys
to the 1966 black Cutlass Supreme
dreaming familiar streets
coasting past crumbling bygone factories
or a wind-swept river
of his youth

The only safe bet
my father knows
are the prescription bottles
on a nearby dresser

He lives for tomorrow

Eye to Eye
After Surgery On My Left Eye

They are twin brothers
suddenly fighting for attention
inside my head
the better one miserable
about having now failed me
the other dancing
like a fool in an open field
happy in his new notoriety
I want to ask
What do you see?
But the two squabble continuously
paying me no heed
lost in tenacious claims
eager to be alone, free
luxuriating in pure autonomy
What do you see?
I demand over and over again
as I make my way
down winding dark staircases
along glaring sun-drenched streets
I need your help
I complain as I slip into a car
to drive across town
worried sick about my safety

One eye finally relinquishes
all concerns, but only for the moment
as he surveys the road itself
and pauses to warn me of the passage
how close the curb is
the colour of lights ahead
Meanwhile the other is off on his own
spots a park where
someone is walking a dog
life is dreamy, solitary

who needs anyone else —
live for the moment
What do you see?
I want to know
but neither is speaking to me
as I zigzag fretfully into the future
uncertain of the very curve of the earth
sensing how my two impetuous sons
try to outdo one another
as they anxiously preen and pirouette
before one another
troubled over whether the world is
actually looking
at them

Woman In The Stone Cottage
For Pat Sturn At Age 100

This morning
I woke from a dream
wherein I was carrying
your cane —
the one you used to hang
over the door handle
to the kitchen

I saw you use it
maybe once
when you asked my wife
to accompany you
on a tour of
your tiny stone cottage

Why was I carrying it?
Or did I? It floated before me
awkwardly out of reach

This morning
I woke from a dream
and the sky above was
a sickly tornado green
wind picking up
and the cane skipped
along like an impetuous child
in front of me

I couldn't keep up
Where was it taking me?
This morning
I woke from a dream
and you were rushing
along in the garden
behind the cottage

and I was trying to follow
with that silly cane
When did your feet
get so fast,
skirt tails fluttering
and you glancing over
your shoulder

Where were you taking me?

I saw you float high above
the rooftops like
a figure out of Chagall
desperate in
my clambering
among chimneys
and the patchwork of shingles

I tried to wake from
that dream hoping
the cane was firmly
in my hand
to take me back
to take me there

War Widow

She bade him goodbye
at the train station down by the river —
in those last seconds before
he stepped onto the train

and ran her right hand
awkwardly over the wool lapel of his uniform
pretending to smooth out a wrinkle

Years later she would tell me
"I knew he wasn't coming back"

She had been married two months
a son growing within her

She bound his letters from the war
with a red elastic band
and tucked them into a dresser drawer

Years later when she married again
there were times when
she would slip these out
and sit for an afternoon
and read them

struggling to make sense
of those years
as a young widow with a baby son

in whose eyes she saw a stolen future

If I Wrote Your Obit
For John B. Lee

As we sweep a tangle of branches
away from the gaping entrances
and step boldly into the cold barns
that sit abandoned
like bad children
I wonder what I might write
about you if I live to see you die

I see two dusty smocks
left dangling on a hook
those of the hired hand
a friend of your father's
dead now maybe 40 years
never taken down

Surely, you don't expect him
to return this gray winter day

Sometimes when I look at you
I see your father
— maybe in the way you lean
on the wooden gate
breath steaming the air
as you speak about
those who peopled this farm

I wonder if deep down
you sense betrayal
in your decision
to pack a bag
at that end of a summer day —
eager eyes seeking city streets
limbs lifting and departing
wind sweeping open fields
or how you rose at dawn to care for lambs
or rode the pickup into town

Do you sense the wrong?
Do you wake wondering
what might've been?
Do you walk into these
tumble-down barns
where nature is doing all it can
to shrug off the weight
of that history?

Did it occur to you
that you might slip on
those tattered coats
that hang in the barn?

The Barrow

His work boots are carefully lined up
under a narrow wooden table
fat jars of anise
bake in the morning sunlight
a calendar with a partly naked woman
hangs near an open window
and time has stopped at November
though it's now July
Denis today is wearing a shirt
not like when we met him
on the sloping field down the road
where his truck was parked
and where he kept a jug of wine
He was full of smiles then
and his large hands gestured
to the sweep of vines
row by row as though
they were his students
in a classroom
Today he settles down
at a table in the Burgundian sunlight
and pours us a drink
and wants to tell us about his pig
and the chickens he keeps
but it is the pig he wants us
to see and guides us
along the gravel pathway
to the barn and unlatches
the heavy wooden door
and the light
of the afternoon floods
the doorway
and Denis steps inside —
his pig circling in the pen
like an excited family dog
Denis stands to one side
as if he is introducing a wife
or a girlfriend and it occurs to me
the woman who earlier placed the glasses

on the table in the garden
was his girlfriend and
he never introduced her
before she took his keys
and drove off in his truck
but here we are with his pig
her flat snout
stretching out for our affection
and Denis is proud in this moment
standing to one side
in the cool darkness of the hot day
This man who speaks
about politics, the rules
the levies on his business
and says the secret is
to keep things simple
hide under the radar
find a way around
make things work out
I imagine at night
before he shuts the door
and returns
to the modest house
he reaches down
and tells the pig
everything that's
on his mind
— disagreements
with municipal bureaucrats
— a woman who visits
each day to have lunch
—neighbours who scorn
his eccentric ways
And why not tell the pig?
The pig sees him
and paces the pen
happy to hear his voice
and never disagrees
and believes him
to be right and wise
Besides, she is always there
to bid him goodnight

Guardian Angel

He's lazy and never around
when I need him
I drive down
to the coffee shop
in the early morning
and find him reading the paper
or talking to the locals

I want to tell him
he's not taking this seriously
— he's supposed to watch over me
He shrugs and says the rules
have changed
I can reach him on Facebook
Besides he carries a cell phone

I want to ask him how he got this job
Why me? Why him?
Luck of the draw, he shrugs
our birthdays the same
we both have bad eyes
a hearing problem
and can't eat spicy foods

But where was he in October 1950
the afternoon on Wyandotte
when I was four
and I ran between
two parked cars?
He was there, he says
coming out of the pool hall
to save me
to cup my bleeding head
on the warm pavement
to glare at the driver
who stood in the open door

of his Ford worried sick
that I might die

He was there, he said
otherwise I might not
be having this conversation
and he was there again
when I lay curled up
and unconscious
in the hospital room one winter
swearing at the hospital staff
after bowel surgery
and he touched my lips
with his index and middle fingers
and quieted me

Besides, he's always there
and there's no point
having this conversation
— he's so far ahead
and knows so much more:
a hundred different languages
names of every star
in the universe, the physics
of flying, and the winner
of the Stanley Cup
every year till the
end of time

No Lazy Bones

I'm no lazy bones,
I'm a busy man, I work all day
the man shouts as he shuffles
in sunlight outside
this sprawling but empty
72-passenger school bus
parked in a desolate church lot
at Michigan and Trumbull

A fire rages in a nearby barbeque pit
as he feeds it cardboard boxes
and Sunday's *Free Press*
and assures me the men will keep warm
huddled tonight around
the back of the bus
that's going nowhere

The word *Democracy*
is emblazoned across
the whole side of the bus
shouts out to the vacant street
and to the man
who roams free in the open space
of this lumbering creature
that looms like T-Rex over
a barren urban landscape

I'm no lazy bones
I'm a busy man, I work all day

The Underpainting
for Ken Saltmarche and Russel Farrow

The young man painted a forest
over the mayor's bedroom walls —
Sumacs, Red Bud, Yellow Birch,
Mulberry, Witch-hazel
Dogwood, and Beech – muted stretches
of branches, green as spring,
and a sky spreading its way as
hands softly through hair
And the young man went away
happy to be paid, and the mayor
woke each day to a dazzling forest
in morning light, and knew
the days were right

After a long while, the mayor
passed away and the house was sold
others came and went
and the forest bloomed each morning
and others woke to its brilliant light
of Yellow Birch, Beech and Mulberry

till another moved in one dull-gray day
maybe spooked by the forest
its branches or the gaps of a clear blue sky
maybe fearful of the past
or ghosts that live in such swirls of green
and so he painted it over

At night — so the story goes,
the mayor and the painter, both long dead
wend their way down the solitary street
and climb the stairs to the upper bedroom
and together hear the wind in the Dogwood
and feel the luster of light

The Innocent

for Peter and Denise Hrastovec

There is nothing you could know
of a boy who sleeps in a dream
and glides with the grace of prayer

My friends, hear his plea,
see the story, see his face
see the streets in which he plays

see the boy who sails on hope
through streets that you don't know

see the boy who glides with ease
of day-long joy, see the dream
that he can't know

see him glide with the grace of prayer
that sets his face aglow

My friends, there is nothing you can see
unless you find the words to say

there's a dream, there's a boy
there's a prayer, there's a way
to find the streets that sing that joy
otherwise glide with the grace of prayer

and find the boy who sleeps in a dream

New Poems

The Magic Wand
For Lucien

The wizard is poised in the room
like a Halloween witch
with that wide-brimmed peaked hat
prattling on like a philosopher
inviting us to feel that invisible ball of energy
vibrating between our outstretched hands

She's here for the launch
of the new Harry Potter book
but my five-year-old grandson is lost
in the magic wand she has placed in his hands
as she speaks about drawing protectives circles
casting spells, warding off dark forces,
even banishing bunions

My grandson marvels at this instrument
whispering feverishly
"Abracadabra…abracadabra…"
—no longer hearing this wizard
who has fashioned this shaman's wand
from an aging oak tree

Instead, he's channeling his own energy
into the room, but it isn't working
Nothing is flying about
No sudden gusts of wind, nor pantry doors
slamming shut, nor rattling teacups in mid air

and nothing bigger than he might imagine:
still poverty, still a need for world peace,
still violence and pestilence and polluted lakes

My grandson is poised and ready
And frantically waves the wand about him
like a symphonic conductor gone mad

yet nothing changes —it won't even silence
this nattering witch from telling us
about Greco Roman wands
or ceremonial fire wands and lotus wands
or those used by the freemasons in
all their ritualistic nonsense
Then suddenly in a dramatic abracadabra ending
my grandson shatters the spell:
"Hey, lady, how does this thing work?"

Men at The Shell Station

It was late fall
and I would see the men at the back of
the Shell Station —a dim light of
the garage interior
the men resting on wooden milk crates
borrowed from the dairy
across the
road — playing poker
a brand new '58 Monarch
on a hoist like a prize stallion
and me and my buddies outside
going around the back to climb
atop a mound of discarded tires
and oil drums
to crouch at a broken window
and listen to the same old stories
mostly talk about women —
never their wives
mostly friends' wives
 — horny little things
who couldn't control themselves
And we'd glance at one another
fearing our own mother's name
might be mentioned
but it never was
and we wouldn't have known
what to do if it was —
our brains stirring with secrets
imagining things
that made no sense to kids
barely 12, and after a while
our hands and feet were freezing
and we'd climb down in darkness
and we'd stand in the street
someone would light up
a crumpled cigarette

scrounged from some dad's ashtray
and we'd take turns smoking it
and marvel at the rings
rising miraculously
in the cold fall air

Mother

I see that girl born
in the back bedroom of that farm
that sits tall on a landscape
that gives itself to rain and sun

I hear her tiny voice
bearing itself clean like an echo
in the upstairs corridors
her mother holding her close

daytime breaking over wheat fields
that furrow the flat terrain
her father's steps on the wooden stairs
as he moves to greet his baby daughter

You would be 100 today
if you had not died at the hospital
on the 5th floor where
the morning sun poured in

I raced up the stairs
and along the corridor to your room

your mouth gaping open
as if to swallow the ceiling above
spectacles on the night table
glimmering with mute sunlight

I was too late to say goodbye

Today I say hello, your birthday
You would be 100

When The Light Gets Warm

When the light gets warm
the world curves
around the Stoney Point farmhouse
where childhood races in sunlight
disappearing into shadows

I am a boy hiding
on my brothers in the henhouse
peering through chicken wire
to the yard with
its shiny bright Buick
I see them running
trying to find me
I am giggling
and the birds
cautiously step away
like 11-year-old girls
walking in an older sister's
high heels

When the light gets warm
I am a boy squatting
in the henhouse
watching the day wind
down, seeing my family
search behind
farm sheds, silos
and along fence rows
I see my mother pushing
back a lock of hair
one hand on her hip
in worry, my father
pacing beside the car
and lighting up a cigarette
my grandmother coming
from the house, the screen door

slapping behind her
wanting the last word

When the light gets warm
they have given up
and no longer call out
and my father slips into the Buick
slams the door and
my brothers pile in one by one
so does my mother
who glances back
one last time
I feel so alone as
I sit in the henhouse
and wonder at my hands
cupping a heart full of melancholy
knowing summer is
turning to twilight

When the light gets warm
I suddenly burst
from the henhouse
my six-year-old legs
sprinting to the Buick
that is now moving
in a cloud of road dust
and I can smell
the fields of wheat
and hear my tiny voice
rising all the way down
to my beating heart
in my chest
then see a back door
opening and a brother's hand
reaching out ...

Table Manners

I'd like to ask that man
at the next table
why he dips his toast
into his mug of hot tea
— something so familiar
about his table manners
He folds and refolds the paper
scanning wars and scandals
weather reports and box scores
doing what he's always done
what his father before him did
what he learned in youth
as he dips the crust
into the tea as naturally
and smoothly as
someone signing a check
I want to ask the man
at the next table
what he does for a living
why he's here at 5 a.m.
Is he going to work?
Is this the end of a shift?
Married? Retired?
What he thinks of the Tigers
losing seven straight,
what might be his
favourite novel, colour
what he thinks of the day
coming alive only just now
as the sky lightens outside
the dark windows
of this coffee shop
I'd like to ask
why he folds the newspaper
so methodically before
he rises to leave and why

he stands there a moment
to drain the last of the tea
and why he goes out
the side door and takes
the route across the parking lot
and what is so familiar
about him as he takes a turn
at a narrow alley way behind
those homes near the fire hall
and why as I see him
disappear into the morning
I realize he could be me
heading home without a reason
in the world to explain
who he is or why
he dips his toast
into his tea

First Hearing Gordon Lightfoot

Maybe the spring of 1967
on a cool Saskatchewan night
I was following the edge of the highway
daydreaming those flat open fields

maybe praying under an ink-black sky
that rested solitary and present over me
like the palm of a hand

when a preacher swerved
to the side of the road
in a dusty green *Plymouth Belvedere*

I spotted the flashing red of the ribbon style taillights
that wrapped around the knife edge crease
running down to the bumper
and heard the man shout if I needed a ride

I hopped in, eager to be on my way
and talk soon turned to Jesus
and forgiveness and morality
and the Psalms
and I asked if he could turn on the radio

That's when I first heard that voice
sailing up and out this preacher's car —
a voice that spun in the still prairie air
the blur of notes like the landscape
whistling by

and I told him to turn up the radio
and that he'd have to stop talking and listen
and said if the apostles had this man's voice
there'd be real hope to cling to

and we wound the windows shut

and grew silent in that sudden moment
seeing the highway stretching clean and straight
beneath us like endless prayer

but we fell silent and alone as
that voice in the wilderness
was taking us somewhere different
somewhere distant

and maybe the dashboard lit up
like a votive lamp — I'm not sure

Room With a Face

For Howard and Jeannette Aster at La Roche D'Hys, France

The room glows
from a storybook quarter moon
that hangs in the window
and the ghost-white cows far below
doze away in the valley
dreaming of tomorrow's
sunshine and rain

and I fall to sleep
seeing the moon
press its face to the glass
wishing it might join me
in this night of stories

I tell it instead to stay where it is
I tell it to wait and see
I tell it to sing me a lullaby
as I wait to fall away free

The room glows
from a storybook quarter moon
I touch its grimacing face
I feel it depart — graceful
and splendid—
soaring into darkness
so the meadow can bloom full of light

I wish myself to sleep
hearing the moon breathe
I sail with it safely into the night sky
the drifting clouds beneath

The room glows
from a storybook quarter moon
and I feel myself lifting into darkness

my limbs soaring among stars
and glimpsing the house
and slumbering cows
in the sleepy meadow below

I tell the moon to whisper its rumours
I tell it to linger and hear
I tell it to sing of its passage
into a place without fear

Windsor's Field of Dreams 1900
Ouellette's Square in the years before
building the Windsor Armouries

It wasn't a perfect field
but the late day light was good
the way it fell

accentuating white
flannel numbered collarless shirts
wool knickers and straw hats

as swarthy players gathered
arriving already by bicycle
others in boxy black vehicles

It wasn't a perfect field
yet it was theirs and the day was good
the way it fell

It wasn't a perfect day
in windy open turf so flat and wide
running their way home

giving them victory
in a fading field of dark shadows
as the day wore on

But the city was dreaming
and other men were coming with blueprints
to break and build the soil

For them it was the perfect field
when the late day light was good
and the field was clean and green

Yet for the players they'll never be perfect men
stepping on to a field no longer there
to run hard as the day wears on

Chasing the Light

I must catch the moon
and run down the beach
to see it clearly
its path across the lake
in a straight line
like someone challenging me
to choose sides

I must catch the moon
as it rises above the forest
to see it clearly
its height stretching for darkness
in the boldest of its reach
like someone waking suddenly
for me to embrace

I must catch the moon
and race down along the river
to see it clearly
its face nodding sleepily
from behind a cloud
like an old man dreaming
the slow spinning of a night sky

I must catch the moon
as it moves like sunlight on a street
to see it clearly
its captive gesture telling me
to trust its graceful dance

On the Occasion of the Tall Ships in Windsor

I hear them sing sea shanties
on long summer days
Topsail schooners and brigantines and brigs
I feel them drift to the sky
full of heartache and dismay
I see these ghostly vessels

I hear their songs
amid spinnaker sails
Topmasts, Square rigs, ketches and sloops
I see them sway
like mirrors of the sea
these solitary yawls
lightweight and taller
I feel them nudge the horizon
and grow dim, and sway
as they skim
across a cloud-drifted lake

I hear them sing sea shanties
on long summer days
fearing faltering three-masted sails
fearing wind, sudden, and picking up
as we hurry to lash down gratings
and cuss looming 12-foot swells
as we dip and plummet headlong
into wet rain like jilted brides

I hear them sing
sea shanties on long summer days
flimsy ketches and sloops and cutters
I see them reef the small sails
as wind mounts a terrible refrain
They sing for this storm
with sullen disdain

I hear them sing
sea shanties on long summer days
simple barges and dinghies and staysail schooners
They sing for the moon
in its flight to deny
They sing till the sea
melts into the sky

The Talking Monk

In this world of silence
he's a monk
who likes to talk non-stop
in the kitchen
where he doesn't
feel like working —
chatterbox in corridors
on the way to choir
motor mouth at matins
blabbermouth,
bigmouth,
babbler,
blowhard
yapper,
gabber
windbag
squealer
a bag of wind,
who doesn't wish
to do anything
really
but talk

Soon the other monks
busy themselves
finding places to hide
from him
things to do

so this rotund monk
sashays outside
having swiped scraps of food
from the kitchen
to feed the raccoons

and when these creatures
tiptoe into his sphere
he speaks to them
tells them what's
on his mind

Soon the cats, too
swarm around
at the end of day
and his voice fills
with excitement

The old gasbag
finally has someone
willing to listen…

Four of Us

There are four of us
who file into this coffee shop each morning
in cool darkness before dawn
We don't know one another
except to nod, and go about our business
silently scanning newspaper headlines
scribbling out puzzling Sudoku answers
teasing the waitresses, maybe arguing over
the fortunes of the Tigers' bullpen
or complaining of weather.
There are days when we should talk
when we have something to say
if only to feel better about it
Days when we wonder
about one another, what we did in life
what we cared about, who we are
Instead we ask nothing of each other
We sit in opposite corners
of the coffee shop, the waitresses
knowing us better maybe than we do ourselves
certainly our preferences —
the man two tables away is a *double double*
the one in the corner is *medium vanilla latte*
the fellow with a stack of newspapers,
extra large black and I'm the only one
who drinks a tea, in a china mug
I guess I'm *Mr. Tea*
Anyway, it was maybe this spring
I realized I hadn't seen
the man two tables away
and so I broke the silence
and asked *medium vanilla latte*
if he knew where he was, maybe
in Florida for the winter, though
other winters he was always here,
or maybe he was trying another coffee shop

and *medium vanilla latte* said *double double*
had been sick, a bad heart, and maybe
he might be coming out soon
that he had been bad, nearly died
on the operating table
and for the first time, we were speaking
one to the other, our words
of sickness, of someone of our group
near death, of something missing
in our morning hours together
in a way of the routine, the balance
the shape of our lives shifting
to something else
that didn't seem right

I'll Call You Jack

Based on the painting "The West Wind" by Tom Thomson

I'll ask you to dance for me
why wait for wind and rain
I'll ask you to sing for me
why tremble over a coming storm
I'll ask you to join me
and seize the cloudy day

take a bow
and move with grace
take a step
in this firm embrace

I'll sing to you
if that helps you lift your weary limbs
I'll dress you in shades of autumn
if you sing forgotten hymns

I'll wait for you to join me
to raise your voice
and dull the wind and rain

I'll ask you to dance with me
when nothing else matters more
I'll wait for you to join me now
above the lake and distant shore

Now leave behind all solemn silence
and dance with me—
I'll wait for you

The Last of the Passenger
Pigeons of Our Lady of Assumption

The black robes are gone
So are the villagers, farmers and soldiers
I have nothing more to say

Yet my wings carry me across
the morning river —
steeples of St. Anne's rising in the mist
signaling to me
like the holy shepherd hand
And I wonder about my brothers & sisters
there roosting under the eaves
away from the coming rain
voices silenced

I have nothing more to say

Yet I see the turmoil among men & women
struggles of war, of famine, of typhoid
hunger and fear

I have nothing more to say

Yet my eyes are clear as I drift
high above a sprawling lazy river
trace the comings and goings
of a people forgotten now
in the chaos of deafening canons
and bloody skirmishes
the scars of political wranglings

I have nothing to say
my ears exploding with the angelus
I am close to heaven
I am a ghost of what was
and I am silent

Sailing in the moody-gray day
my wings lifting with the weight of history
my head bursting with philosophies
my tongue alive with language

I have nothing more to say
I see, and I am mute
I sail and I am silent

I have a voice that may sing
soaring high about the steeple's mysteries
that define the pure frailty of God

And now I rise above the generations
of others, and float above
the miraculous blue of this sleeping river

believing in nothing more
than one final single flight that signals
the end of a long day

When there's no reason to speak

I see, and I am mute
I sail and I am silent
I am nothing more

The Road We Take

Here's the road we take
in all the hapless wandering
Beneath the sun the moon the sky
Here's the way to mind
the stars that fill the lake

Here's all we need for wandering
knowing there's a melody in this journey
a song to gather voices
where words bring us closer
and take us far
where our limbs, like branches, stretch
to catch the metaphors

Here's all we need for wandering
We have words and yearnings
and feel ourselves stretch to catch the night
and see the morning rise
Here's all we need
to nudge the melody beneath our feet
to take us far and find the magic
in all that lives beneath the sun the moon the sky

The Boy Near The Window
Inspired by a WWII story from France

I lay by the window
staring up at the night sky
and the dizziness of stars that swarm
over the farmhouse and barn
and courtyard

I am a boy again
where night bleeds
in the moonlight's memory
and feel the fury of that morning
when they brought the soldiers
to the farmer's wife
and shot them in the yard

I am a boy again
who lives with this story
knowing they are buried
somewhere in that slope
behind the barn

I am a boy again
and feel them
just beyond my window
believe I hear their voices
in the courtyard

I want to tell them
let your bones lift out
of the dark earth
fearful and bewildered

I want to tell them
turn your faces to the night sky
forget everything
let it go

About the author

Photo courtesy of Dax Melmer, *Windsor Star*

Marty Gervais is an award-winning journalist, photographer, poet, playwright, historian, editor, and teacher. In 1998, he won the prestigious Toronto's Harbourfront Festival Prize for his contributions to Canadian letters and to emerging writers. In 1996, he was awarded the Milton Acorn People's Poetry Award for his book, Tearing Into A Summer Day. That book was awarded the City of Windsor Mayor's Award for literature. Table Manners is the companion volume to *To Be Now: new and selected poems 1989 – 2003* which was awarded the City of Windsor Mayor's Award for literature. Marty was named the inaugural Poet Laureate of Windsor, Ontario.